MEDIA COVERAGE OF TERRORISM

Methods of Diffusion

A. Odasuo Alali
Kenoye Kelvin Eke
editors

SAGE PUBLICATIONS
The International Professional Publishers
Newbury Park   London   New Delhi

For information address:

SAGE Publications, Inc.
2455 Teller Road
Newbury Park, California 91320

SAGE Publications Ltd.
6 Bonhill Street
London EC2A 4PU
United Kingdom

SAGE Publications India Pvt. Ltd.
M-32 Market
Greater Kailash I
New Delhi 110 048 India

Printed in the United States of America

Library of Congress Cataloging-in-Publication Data

Main entry under title:

Media coverage of terrorism : methods of diffusion / edited by A.
    Odasuo Alali and Kenoye Kelvin Eke.
        p.   cm. — (Sage focus editions   ; v.   130.)
    Includes bibliographical references and index.
    ISBN 0-8039-4190-0 (cloth). — ISBN 0-8039-4191-9 (pbk.)
        1. Terrorism in the press—United States—History—20th century.
2. Terrorism in the press—Great Britain—History—20th century.
3. Terrorism in mass media—20th century. 4. Terrorism—Political
aspects. 5. Press—Objectivity. 6. Telecommunication—Social
aspects—20th century. I. Alali, A. Odasuo, 1957- . II. Eke,
Kenoye Kelvin.
PN4784.T45M4 1991
303.6′25—dc20   90-28310
                                                                            CIP

FIRST PRINTING, 1991

Sage Production Editor: Astrid Virding

Contents

Preface

Although terrorism has for a long time been used as an instrument of control and warfare by states, and as an instrument of subversion by groups seeking to change a particular political order, it did not receive much attention from academics, governments, or the mass media. This picture was to change in the 1970s and 1980s for a number of reasons. A partial list of the causes of this change would include the following: an increase in the number of groups that believed in the profitability of terrorism as a means of changing the status quo; a substantial increase in the incidents of terrorism committed against Western targets; the proliferation of technological know-how on explosives manufacturing; and, perhaps most importantly, the recent advancements in telecommunications technology, which have increased both the size of the audience and the speed with which news and information travel.

Along with this change from benign neglect to a reasonable diffusion of news on terrorist events has come a concern for the role of the mass media in this diffusion. This concern has mostly been expressed in the form of questions on whether or not media coverage of terrorism has a contagion effect. There have also been questions raised on what the proper role of the media, especially television, ought to be.

1

Unfortunately, for students of terrorism and those of us who teach courses on this phenomenon, these questions are heard the loudest in the period immediately following a high-profile terrorist event and subside shortly thereafter. Consequently, there is a paucity of literature on the subject matter. This book attempts to fill the void that exists on the comprehensive treatment of these and other questions concerning the media and terrorism. We have assembled in this book what we believe are excellent analyses of specific aspects of the media's role in the diffusion of news on terrorism.

We wish to thank our friends at Sage Publications, especially our sponsoring editor Ann West and editorial assistant Marie Louise Penchoen, for their support and patience. We also wish to thank Professors Marla Iyasere of California State University, Bakersfield, Hashim Gibrill of Clark Atlanta University, Cecil Blake of Howard University, and Ja A. Jahannes of Savannah State College for reviewing the manuscript; and Idowu Oladejo Ibrahim for typing part of the manuscript.

We wish to acknowledge the partial financial support for this project that came, via a grant, from California State University, Bakersfield.

Finally, we acknowledge our indebtedness to those who have played active roles in our intellectual and personal growth. They include: Laura Ann Fleet, Solomon Iyasere, Robert Nwankwo, Annette Brock, Hanes Walton Jr., James Powell, Joy G. Eke, K. J. Kelvin-Eke, and our past and current students. It is to them that this book is dedicated.

— *A. Odasuo Alali*
Kenoye Kelvin Eke

1

Introduction

Critical Issues in Media Coverage of Terrorism

KENOYE KELVIN EKE
A. ODASUO ALALI

The proliferation and intensity of incidents of terrorism in the 1970s and 1980s earned terrorism the attention of scholars, government officials, and the mass media. This attention has resulted in the publication of studies on the why and how of terrorism, and the type of individuals and groups who commit terrorist acts by academics and journalists alike (Flyn & Gerhardt, 1990; Melman, 1989). While these studies have dealt with terrorism in all of its complexities, there is yet to be an agreement on what terrorism is. This lack of definitional consensus on terrorism is important not only to academics, who need it for scholastic veracity, but also for the media, which as an institution play an important role in the characterization or labeling of acts of political violence. The definition of terrorism has an impact on whether or not the perpetrators of an act of violence are labeled "criminals," "terrorists," or "freedom fighters." It is especially important given that media's choice of label in their coverage of an act of violence stands to influence, tremendously, the audience's perceptions of the perpetrators of the act.

The Problematique of Defining Terrorism

While consensus has eluded scholars, there has not been any reluctance on their part to understand terrorism. One such effort is that of

3

Walter Laqueur (1987, pp. 11-12) who, in his book *The Age of Terrorism*, grapples with the intricacies of the term *terrorism* and the label *terrorist* as he traces their origin and meaning over the years to contemporary usage. In his view terrorism has undergone changes in character over the last century and these changes compound the definitional problems one faces in dealing with it.

Understanding terrorism has meant trying to define it. One of the most serious attempts to define terrorism has been that of Paul Wilkinson (1974). First Wilkinson makes a distinction between four types of terrorism (criminal, psychic, war, and political) before defining political terrorism as "the systematic use or threat of violence to secure political ends" (p. 17). He further distinguishes political terrorism into three broad types: "revolutionary," "subrevolutionary," and "repressive." According to Wilkinson the first type, revolutionary terrorism, is a systematic use of violence with the ultimate goal being to obtain a radical change in the political order. The second type, subrevolutionary terrorism, is the use of terroristic violence to effect a change in public policy without altering the political order. The third type, repressive terrorism, involves the use of violence to suppress or restrain certain individuals or groups from forms of behavior considered undesirable by the state (pp. 36-40). Whereas the first two types are used by individuals and nonstate actors against target states, the latter is used by states to maintain a status quo that may be advantageous to those belonging to a particular class, ethnic or racial group, or religious faith. States that practice this form of terrorism usually explain their repressive actions as being in the interest of national security even though the real purpose of their actions may have been to maintain regime security. South Africa is a good example of a nation in which this form of terrorism is practiced.

In his contribution to our understanding of terrorism, Andrew Pierre (1984) focuses on terrorism of the international variety. Although conceding the difficulty of endowing international terrorism with a universally acceptable definition, he sees it as "acts of violence outside national boundaries, or with clear international repercussions" (p. 85). He goes on to list factors that motivate international terrorists. According to him:

(1) The terrorist is dedicated to a political goal which he sees as one of transcendent merit. . . .

(2) The terrorist seeks attention and publicity for his cause. . . .

(3) The terrorist aims to erode support for the established political leader-
     ship or to undermine the authority of the state by destroying normality,
     creating uncertainty, polarizing a country, fostering economic discord
     and generally weakening the fabric of society. . . .

(4) The terrorist's actions can be a measure of deep frustration where there
     is no legitimate way to redress grievances. . . .

(5) The terrorist may seek to liberate his colleagues in foreign jails. . . .

(6) Finally, the terrorist may desire money so as to buy arms and finance
     his organization. (pp. 86-87)

Further, Pierre (p. 85) is of the opinion that international terrorism is
usually but not exclusively carried out by nonstate actors.

Implicit in discussions of international terrorism of the type presented by Pierre is that there is terrorism of a domestic variety. Although there have been relatively fewer incidents of domestic terrorism in the United States, according to a recent study by Bruce
Hoffman (n.d., p. 1), there are groups in the United States whose
motives for acts of violence are similar to those of groups engaged in
international terrorism (pp. 3-8).

The difficulty identified by Pierre (1984) of defining international
terrorism is not unique to scholars. The same problem has plagued the
efforts of U.S. government officials and agencies in defining international terrorism. However, in this case, the definitional problem
and confusion pertains mostly to the sponsorship of these acts
(Bernstein, 1986, pp. 149-167; Casey, 1986, pp. 59-72; Motley, 1987,
pp. 15-23). This is manifested in the fact that although the
Departments of State, Defense, and Justice and the Central Intelligence Agency (CIA) and Federal Bureau of Investigation (FBI) all
have issued definitions of terrorism that are couched in terms of the
use of violence, intimidation, or force as the means to a political end,
there are differences in their interpretations. Each tends to be selective in the way it interprets acts of political violence. Their interpretations of terrorism seem to be motivated by each agency's objectives relevant to policy or use of resources. For instance, the State
Department officially defines terrorism as "the threat or use of violence for political purposes by individuals or groups whether acting
for or in opposition to established governmental authority when such
actions are intended to shock, stun, or intimidate a target group wider
than the immediate victims" (Treisman, 1986, p. 91). This definition
has been conveniently interpreted to exclude nonstate groups (such

as the counter revolutionaries or Contras in Nicaragua) and agents of the state (such as the U.S.-trained Atlacatt battalion of El Salvador's army) that have allegedly committed terroristic acts (pp. 91-96).

Conversely, nonstate actors and nation-states whose ideological views are at variance with those espoused by top government officials and agencies are conferred with the pejorative label *terrorists* or *practitioners of state-sponsored terrorism,* as the case may be. The State Department's list of terrorists and sponsors of terrorism has typically included the Palestine Liberation Organization (PLO), and cited Libya, Iran, Syria, and North Korea as supporters of terrorism (Shultz, 1986, pp. 49-55). This list can be shortened or lengthened as foreign policy imperatives demand. That was the case recently when the U.S. response to the Persian Gulf crisis demanded the addition of Iraq, after it invaded Kuwait on August 2, 1990, to the list while Syria's alleged role as a supporter of terrorism was being downplayed by the State Department (Friedman, 1990, p. A16).

Apparently, defining terrorism is like a chimera. The complexity of the term not only has created definitional problems for society, but also has confused and indeed polluted the debate on how to characterize acts of political violence. This leads us to pose the question: When is an act of political violence an act of terrorism, and when is it a legitimate instrument of struggle for a people determined to escape a political cul-de-sac? Differently put, when is one accurate in labeling an act of violence, an individual, or group *terrorist,* and when should the more sympathetic label *freedom fighter(s)* be conferred on an actor or group of actors?

Thus far, the literature suggests to us that labelling acts of political violence is situationally dependent and idiosyncratic—it depends on who is being labeled and the party doing the labeling (Chomsky, 1986, pp. 1-6). There is no doubt that the choice of label has implications and is therefore very important to those who cover violent political events: the media, and the consumers of the news they cover—the audience which, thanks to technological innovations, is being globalized.

In this book, we present the reader with two chapters on characterization and labeling. The analysis by Robert Picard and Paul Adams in Chapter 2 focuses on characterization by three elite U.S. dailies: the *Los Angeles Times,* the *New York Times,* and the *Wash-*

ington Post. The discussion by Brian Simmons in Chapter 3 analyzes labeling as done by U.S. newsmagazines.

Media Coverage and Its Consequences

The media interest in terrorism that we alluded to earlier, manifested in increased coverage of terrorist events, has brought on a new debate. This debate on whether or not media coverage of terrorist events encourages "terrorists" to carry out more such acts has not only involved media personnel, but has also received the attention of academics. However, before we discuss this debate, let's first examine the nature of media coverage of terrorism. Doing this dictates that we look at the methods of diffusion of news, stories, and other programs on terrorism, and the functions that the media perform.

The two broad methods of disseminating information on terrorism are through the electronic media and the print media. The electronic media comprise radio, over-the-air television, and cable television, and the print media include newspapers and newsmagazines. Of these methods of diffusion television is the most pervasive and profound. It is the primary source of news and entertainment for the average American (Graber, 1989, p. 3). Television's premier position as the primary source of news for Americans will not be challenged by any of the other methods any time soon given the ever-increasing penetration of cable and satellite television into the American culture. The attractiveness of cable as a delivery system for news as well as entertainment has resulted in it penetrating over 50% of American households (pp. 376-378). This penetration is significant and especially germane to our focus because cable outlets such as Cable News Network (CNN), with their news orientation and resultant ability to get reporters on the scene of a news event quickly, can afford to do in-depth coverage of terrorist events. In-depth news coverage is not unique to CNN—the newspapers, newsmagazines, and television networks provide this kind of coverage but usually only in crisis situations. The clamor for the scoop and in-depth coverage in crisis situations tend to lead to what Doris Graber (1989) calls "pack journalism." According to Graber (pp. 315-316), pack journalism often leads to inaccuracies in reportage being replicated throughout the media. In Chapters 6, 7, and 8, we present case studies done by three scholars (Tony Atwater, John Viera, and Jack Lule, respectively) on the different forms that media coverage of terrorism take.

Although the methods of diffusion may differ, there are a set of functions that the media as an institution perform. These functions may impact on the roles that individual media personnel play in their coverage of terrorism. Graber (1989), à la Harold Laswell, believes that the media performs three major functions. These functions are: (a) surveillance (public and private) for the purpose of spotlighting and publicizing ongoing events on the world stage; (b) interpreting the meaning as well as consequences of various events; and (c) serving as an agent of political socialization of the dominant values of the society (pp. 5-11). Graber expands this Laswellian typology to include manipulation as a fourth function being served by the media through their use of muckraking to generate information that will impact on the political process (p. 12). Perhaps there are grounds for one to quarrel or disagree with Graber's fourth function, but not many grounds exist for disagreement with her first three functions. It has been argued, as the discussion in Chapter 4 by Robert Picard will attest, that journalists' perception of their function influence their coverage of news, especially when that news is about terrorism.

Whereas there seems to be no argument about the impact of media coverage of news on its audiences, the same is not true concerning its impact on "terrorists." On this matter, there are two schools of thought. Proponents of the first school contend that media coverage of terrorist events has a contagion effect. According to a leading proponent of this school of thought, Brian Jenkins (1983), "Terrorism is a product of freedom, particularly, of freedom of the press" (p. 160). Another proponent of this school of thought, Yonah Alexander (1979), argues that a consequence of extensive media coverage of terrorism "is the exportation of violent techniques which, in turn, often triggers similar extreme actions by other individuals and groups" (p. 336). Aside from the contagion criticism, other criticisms have been leveled against the media. They range from romanticizing terror to the media as participants, albeit with television cameras, in terrorist events (Livingstone, 1982, pp. 62-71).

The arguments of the proponents of contagion theory are countered by those of a group we shall call the "non-believers," for the lack of a better label. Those who oppose contagion theory tend to share Grant Wardlaw's (1989) position that "there is no clear evidence that publicity (by the media) is responsible for significantly affecting the occurrence of terrorism" (p. 78). As our contribution to this ongoing debate, we offer you Robert Picard's essay, "News Coverage as the Contagion of Terrorism: Dangerous Charges Backed by Dubious Science," as Chapter 5. Picard's discussion puts him squarely within the ranks of the non-believers.

The Media and Counterterrorist Strategy

With many government officials believing that media coverage of terrorism has a contagion effect, it comes as no surprise that the media are seen as having an important role to play in any effort to combat terrorism. Another group that takes a similar position is the contagion theorists. In fairness to contagion theorists, however, expectations of a media role in an effective counterterrorist strategy have not been limited to them; even the non-believers concede a role for the media in view of their symbiotic relation with terrorists and terrorism. The crucial questions that separate these groups, however, are: exactly what form should the media's role take? And at whose behest should the necessary policing of the media come?

On the first question, suggestions for a media role involve some type of news management—a euphemism for censorship, some argue. News management could take different forms, ranging from the media being limited in their coverage of terrorism to its surveillance function and not engaging in interpretations, all the way to news suppression, either temporary or permanent. The harshest of these measures—news suppression especially of the permanent type—has aptly received the loudest criticisms because it is at odds with the glasnost that is pivotal to a democratic society. This conflict with democratic principles has earned a measure of disdain from some media personnel such as Ted Koppel, who while moderating a panel on "Terrorism and the Media" posed the question to the panelists: "Does one oppose terrorism by using methods that are non-democratic—such as censoring the press—or by so doing does one undermine democracy itself?" (Anzovin, 1986, pp. 96-108).

The clash with democratic principles aside, news management, especially of the extreme variety, raises the question of practicability. The question is whether it is realistic to expect industrywide conformity given the competitiveness, both individual and organizational, that characterizes the industry.

Like the previous issues, the question of who should do the policing of the media's role is not devoid of controversy. The controversy on this matter centers on whether the government should provide guidelines for the media's coverage of terrorism, or whether the industry should engage in self-restraint in order to avoid the former. While law enforcement officials and other government officials in agencies concerned with terrorism would like to see government regulation, the sentiments among media personnel seem to favor self-policing as a preemptive action against any legislative policy or government intervention (Anzovin, 1986, p. 105). In keeping with these sentiments many news-gathering organizations and television networks have devised voluntary guidelines to govern coverage of terrorist events by their reporters. Prominent among the television networks that have adopted these types of guidelines is CBS (Dominick, 1990, p. 554; Livingstone, 1982, p. 74). Given the economic milieu in which the media operate, is optimism regarding compliance with self-generated guidelines warranted? We are not certain.

If our discussion in this chapter did not settle any of the issues, it was intentional. It was not our aim to lay to rest any of the issues raised in our discussion; instead, our aim was to remind our readers of some of the critical issues concerning the media and their role in the coverage of terrorism. We hope that our discussion and the contributions included in this book by the scholars of media coverage mentioned previously, along with that from Kevin Barnhurst in Chapter 9, give you food for thought.

References

Alexander, Y. (1979). Terrorism, the media, and the police. In R. Kupperman & D. Trent, *Terrorism: Threat, reality, response* (p. 336). Stanford, CA: Hoover Institution Press.

Anzovin, S. (Ed.) (1986). *Terrorism*. New York: H. W. Wilson.

Bernstein, A. (1986, Spring). Iran's low-intensity war against the United States. *Orbis*, pp. 149-167.

Casey, W. (1986). International terrorism: Potent challenge to American intelligence. In Steven Anzovin (Ed.), *Terrorism* (pp. 59-72). New York: H. W. Wilson.

Chomsky, N. (1986). *Pirates & emperors: International terrorism in the real world.* Brattleboro, VT: Amana.

Dominick, J. R. (1990). *The dynamics of mass communication.* New York: McGraw-Hill.

Flyn, K., & Gerhardt, G. (1989). *The silent brotherhood: Inside America's racist underground.* New York: Free Press.

Friedman, T. L. (1990). Baker will go to Syria for help against Iraqis. *New York Times,* September 11, p. A16.

Graber, D. A. (1989). *Mass media and American politics* (3rd ed). Washington, DC: CQ Press.

Hoffman, B. (n.d.). *Recent trends and future prospects of terrorism in the United States.* Santa Monica, CA: Rand Corporation.

Jenkins, B. (1983). Research in terrorism: Areas of consensus, areas of ignorance. In E. Burr, D. Soskis, and W. Reid (Eds.) *Terrorism: Inter-disciplinary perspectives* (p. 160). Washington, DC: American Psychiatric Association.

Laqueur, W. (1987). *The age of terrorism.* Boston: Little, Brown.

Livingstone, N. C. (1982). *The war against terrorism.* Lexington, MA: Lexington.

Melman, Y. (1986). *The master terrorist: The true story of Abu-Nidal.* New York: Adama.

Motley, J. B. (1987, Fall). Low intensity conflict: Global challenges. *Teaching Political Science.*

Pierre, A. J. (1984). The politics of international terrorism. In C. Kegley and E. Wittkopt (Eds.), *The global agenda* (p. 85). New York: Random House.

Shultz, G. (1986). Terrorism: The challenge to the democracies. In S. Anzovin (Ed.), *Terrorism* (pp. 49-55). New York: H. W. Wilson.

Treisman, D. (1986). Terror error. In S. Anzovin (Ed.), *Terrorism* (p. 91). New York: H. W. Wilson.

Wardlaw, G. (1989). *Political terrorism: Theory, tactics, and counter-measures* (2nd ed). New York: Cambridge University Press.

Wilkinson, P. (1974). *Political terrorism.* London: Macmillan.

2

Characterizations of Acts and Perpetrators of Political Violence in Three Elite U.S. Daily Newspapers

ROBERT G. PICARD
PAUL D. ADAMS

This study considers the characterization of acts of political violence, commonly referred to as terrorism, in the *Los Angeles Times*, the *New York Times*, and the *Washington Post* for the years of 1980 through 1985. The study was undertaken to explore characterizations of acts of political violence and their perpetrators. The study considers the most frequently used characterizations and whether they differ depending upon their source.

Characterizations were dichotomized into the categories of nominal and descriptive, depending upon their meaning. Nominal characterizations are nouns, verbal nouns (gerunds), or other words that label or describe the acts in a manner that merely indicates what happened. They are also words that label or describe the perpetrators, but with as little connotative meaning as possible. Nominal words are straightforward description with as few judgmental qualities about the acts or perpetrators as possible. Descriptive characterizations are often adjectival in form, although they may be nouns or verbal nouns, and contain judgments about the acts or perpetrators within their denotative or connotative meanings.

AUTHORS' NOTE: Reprinted with permission from *Political Communication and Persuasion*, Vol. 4 (1987).

Nominal characterizations of acts of political violence include words such as *hijacker, bombing, shooting,* and *attack.* Nominal characterizations of perpetrators of such acts include words such as *hijacker(s), bomber(s), gunman(men),* and *attacker(s).* Descriptive characterizations of acts of political violence include words such as *murder, despicable, brutal, criminal,* and *terrorism.* Descriptive characterizations of perpetrators of political violence include words such as *murderer(s), criminal(s), coward(s), freedom fighter(s),* and *terrorist(s).*

Method

Incidents selected for inclusion in this study were selected from among entries in the newspaper indices for the three papers using a quota sampling procedure. Because no single comprehensive listing of terrorist acts in the period exists, or is readily available from intelligence agencies, the universe from which the final incidents were selected included incidents of political violence listed under the index headings of assassinations, airline hijackings, bombings, hostages, kidnappings, murders, shootings, and terrorism. The incidents included in the study were randomly selected from among those listed under each heading.

The chosen articles about each incident were individually read and questionnaires completed for each of the articles. A total of 258 reports of 127 incidents of political violence were collected and analyzed for this study. For each story, coders recorded the first three characterizations of acts of political violence and perpetrators of political violence made in quotes attributed to government officials and witnesses, as well as the first three nonquoted characterizations of the acts and perpetrators (i.e., characterizations made by the writer) and characterizations of the acts and perpetrators made in headlines.

Prior to implementing the questionnaire, inter-coder reliability tests were made using the instrument. In tests using the Holsti inter-coder reliability formula, ten paired sets of coders achieved an average reliability of .98, an indication of very high inter-coder reliability.

After the characterizations were gathered, 10 coders were asked to place each characterization found in the articles into either the nominal or descriptive category, based on the operational definitions given

Table 2.1 Combined Characterizations of Acts

Rank	Characterization Word	Number of Uses	Percentage of Total
1	Hijacking	142	15.3
2	Killing	97	10.4
3	Bombing	89	9.6
4	Explosion	88	9.5
5	Attack	59	6.3
6	Blast	54	5.8
7	Shooting	41	4.4
8	Seizure	38	4.1
9	Assassination	21	2.3
10	Slaying	19	2.0
11	Commandeered	17	1.8
12	Hostage taking	17	1.8
13	Threat	14	1.5
14	Ambush	13	1.4
15	Siege	12	1.3

above, to create the list (Appendix 2.1) of nominal and descriptive terms so their use could be analyzed in this study.

Results

A combined total of 931 characterizations of the acts (i.e., events) of political violence were recorded. The five most frequently appearing characterizations were (in order) the words *hijacking, killing, bombing, explosion,* and *attack* (Table 2.1). The five characterizations alone accounted for 51.1% of the total.

The second five most frequently used characterization words to describe the acts were (in order) *blast, shooting, seizure, assassination,* and *slaying*. These five terms accounted for 18.6% of the total, bringing the total accounted for by the 10 terms to 69.7%.

The remaining characterization words that accounted for at least 1% of the total ranked 11th through 15th on frequency of appearance and included 7.8% of the total characterizations. The 15 characterization words accounted for 77.5% of the 931 characterization words recorded.

A combined total of 589 characterizations of the perpetrators were recorded in the study. The five most frequent characterization words

Table 2.2 Combined Characterizations of Perpetrators

Rank	Characterization	Number of Uses	Percentage of Total
1	Hijacker(s)	159	27.0
2	Gunman(men)	76	12.9
3	Guerrilla(s)	55	9.3
4	Terrorist(s)	54	9.2
5	Rebel(s)	31	5.3
6	Leftist(s), Left-wing	23	3.9
7	Armed man(men)	14	2.4
8	Attacker(s)	12	2.0
9	Extremist(s)	12	2.0
10	Rightist(s), Right-wing	7	1.2
11	Nationalist(s)	7	1.2

used for the perpetrators were (in order) *hijacker(s)*, *gunman(men)*, *guerilla(s)*, *terrorist(s)*, and *rebel(s)* (Table 2.2). The five top-ranked terms accounted for 63.7% of the total number of characterizations of perpetrators of political violence.

Six additional terms each accounted for at least 1% of the total number of perpetrator characterizations. The words ranked 12th through 16th. These words were *leftist(s)*, or *left-wing*, *armed man(men)*, *attacker(s)*, *extremist(s)*, *rightist(s)*, or *right-wing*, and *nationalist(s)*. Together these accounted for 12.7% of the total number of characterizations of the perpetrators of the acts of political violence, bringing the total for all terms accounting for at least 1% to 76.4% of the total.

The data were then separated by the source of the characterizations. Headlines and nonquoted material were included in a category of media characterizations, and classifications for government and witness characterizations were also considered.

A total of 858 characterizations of the acts of political violence were made by the media. The top five characterizations were *hijacking*, *killing*, *bombing*, *explosion*, and *attack* (Table 2.3). The top five words used accounted for 54.9% of the total media characterizations.

The 6- through 10-ranked words were *seizure*, *blast*, *shooting*, *assassination*, and *slaying*. The five words in this group accounted for 18.5% of the media total, bringing the percentage of the total resulting from characterizations ranked 1 through 10 to 73.4%.

Table 2.3 Combined Characterizations of Acts

Rank	Characterization	Number of Uses	Percentage of Total
1	Hijacking	142	16.6
2	Killing	95	11.1
3	Bombing	85	9.9
4	Explosion	78	9.1
5	Attack	70	8.2
6	Seizure	52	6.1
7	Blast	34	3.9
8	Shooting	33	3.8
9	Assassination	21	2.5
10	Slaying	19	2.2
11	Commandeered	17	2.0
12	Hostage taking	17	2.0
13	Threat	14	1.6
14	Ambush	13	1.5
15	Siege	12	1.4

Table 2.4 Combined Characterizations of Perpetrators

Rank	Characterization	Number of Uses	Percentage of Total
1	Hijacker(s)	149	28.4
2	Gunman(men)	72	13.7
3	Terrorist(s)	4	7.8
4	Guerrilla(s)	40	7.6
5	Rebel(s)	31	5.9
6	Leftist(s), Left-wing	22	4.2
7	Extremist(s)	21	4.0
8	Armed man(men)	14	2.7
9	Commando(s)	12	2.3
10	Attacker(s)	10	1.9
11	Nationalist(s)	7	1.3

An additional five media characterizations each represented more than 1% of the total. These terms added 8.5% to the total number of media characterizations of the acts, bringing the total to 81.9%.

A total of 525 characterizations were made in the media of the perpetrators of the acts of violence. The top five characterizations were *hijackers*, *gunman(men)*, *terrorist(s)*, *guerrilla(s)*, and *rebel(s)* (Table 2.4). These five words accounted for 63.4% of the total media characterizations.

The words ranked 6 through 10 were *leftist(s)*, or *left-wing*, *extremist(s)*, *armed man(men)*, *commando(s)*, and *attackers*. These characterizations accounted for 15.1% of the total and bring the total for terms ranked 1 through 10 to 78.5%. One additional term, *nationalist(s)*, accounted for at least 1%, bringing the total accounted for by each term above the 1% threshold to 79.8% of all media characterizations.

The portion of the data indicating the characterizations of the acts of political violence in the quoted words of government officials yielded 41 responses. The most prevalent characterization, accounting for nearly 15% of the total, was *criminal (act)*. The second ranked response was *attack*, and the third rank was held by five words with equal number of uses, *bombing*, *brutal act*, *seizure*, *shooting*, and *terrorism* (Table 2.5). These seven terms accounted for 51.3% of the total government officials' characterizations of the acts. Remaining were single responses unduplicated by any other officials' characterizations. Included in the remaining responses were *barbaric*, *cowardly*, *dastardly*, and *despicable*.

Forty-one quoted characterizations by government officials of perpetrators of acts were also recorded. *Hijacker(s)* received the number one rank, accounting for 14.6% of the total (Table 2.6). The second most frequent characterization of the perpetrators was a tie between *terrorist(s)* and *evil*. These terms together accounted for 14.6% of the total. Three terms tied for the fourth ranked characterization: The terms *brutal*, *criminals*, and *rightist(s)*, or *right-wing* totaled an additional 14.7% bringing the total for the characterizations of perpetrators used at least twice by government officials to 43.9%. Responses used only once included characterizations such as *cowards*, *extremists*, and *armed propaganda unit*.

Thirty-three characterizations of the acts were made by witnesses quoted in the news stories. The most frequently used characterization was *explosion*, which accounted for 21.2% of the total (Table 2.7). The second most used characterization was *shooting*, which accounted for 18.2%. Together the two terms contributed 39.4% to the total. The third most frequent characterization was *blast*, which accounted for 12.1% of the total. Two characterizations, *bombing* and

Table 2.5 Government Characterizations of Acts

Rank	Characterization	Number of Uses	Percentage of Total
1	Criminal Act	6	14.6
2	Attack	5	12.2
3	Bombing	2	4.9
4	Brutal Act	2	4.9
5	Seizure	2	4.9
6	Shooting	2	4.9
7	Terrorism	2	4.9

Table 2.6 Witness Characterizations of Perpetrators

Rank	Characterization	Number of Uses	Percentage of Total
1	Hijacker(s)	6	14.6
2	Terrorist(s)	3	7.3
3	Evil	3	7.3
4	Brutal	2	4.9
5	Criminals	2	4.9
6	Rightist(s), Right-wing	2	4.9

seizure, tied for the fourth position, each amounting to 6.1% of the total.

Eighteen characterizations of the perpetrators were made by witnesses quoted in the articles. Only two terms were used multiple times, and they were used an equal amount. *Gunman(men)* and *hijacker(s)* each contributed 22.2% of the total number of characterizations of perpetrators made by witnesses (Table 2.8).

Examination of whether media, government, and witness characterizations differed significantly was made using the chi-square statistic. The pattern of characterization use by the three groups was shown to be highly significant ($p < .001$; Table 2.9). Both media and witness characterizations tended to be nominal. In contrast, the majority of characterizations made by government officials were descriptive.

Because most characterizations were made by media, the kinds of characterizations were compared to determine if there were differences

Table 2.7 Witness Characterizations of Acts

Rank	Characterization	Number of Uses	Percentage of Total
1	Explosion	7	21.2
2	Shooting	6	18.2
3	Blast	4	12.1
4	Bombing	2	6.1
5	Seizure	2	6.1

Table 2.8 Witness Characterizations of Perpetrators

Rank	Characterization	Number of Uses	Percentage of Total
1	Gunman(men)	4	22.2
2	Hijacker(s)	4	22.2

between the characterization of acts and perpetrators. One would expect no association between nominal and descriptive words and the object of the characterization. Using the chi-square statistical test, however, it was revealed that a significant difference ($p < .001$) between media characterization of acts and perpetrators existed (Table 2.10). The data show that media characterizations tended to employ nominal words to characterize acts of political violence to a much greater degree than they did to characterize perpetrators. More than a third of the time, media characterizations of perpetrators employed descriptive terms.

Differences in characterizations of acts of political violence and perpetrators of political violence could not be measured individually for government officials and witnesses because the number of characterizations in each of the cells would be below statistically acceptable thresholds due to the small n for their characterizations.

Summary

This study reveals that a significant difference exists in the ways media personnel, government officials, and witnesses characterize acts of political violence and the perpetrators of those acts. Media personnel

Table 2.9 Summary of Characterizations of Acts and Perpetrators

Source of Characterizations	Nominal Characterizations	Descriptive Characterizations	Totals
Media	927 (83%)	194 (17%)	1121 (94.3%)
Government	17 (44%)	22 (56%)	39 (3.3%)
Witnesses	29 (100%)	0 (00%)	29 (2.4%)
Totals	973 (81.8%)	216 (18.2%)	1189

$\chi^2 = 40.21$, df = 2, $p < .001$

Table 2.10 Summary of Media Characterizations

Object of Characterizations	Nominal Characterizations	Descriptive Characterizations	Totals
Acts	670 (95%)	32 (5%)	702 (62.6%)
Perpetrators	257 (61%)	162 (39%)	419 (37.4%)
Totals	927 (83%)	194 (17%)	1121 (100%)

$\chi^2 = 103.5$, df = 1, $p < .001$

and witnesses to the violence tend to use nominal characterizations, and government officials tend to use descriptive characterizations.

Media personnel and witnesses thus tend to use terms that are generally more neutral than those used by government officials. Government officials tend to use words that are more judgmental, inflammatory, and sensationalistic. A noteworthy finding of this study was that witness characterizations were completely nominal. When considering differences in characterizations made by media personnel, a significant difference was found between characterizations of acts of political violence and characterizations of perpetrators of political violence. Although media personnel tended to use nominal words to characterize acts, they used descriptive characterizations for perpetrators about a third of the time.

No readily available explanation for this difference is apparent, although an examination of the words seems to show that they do not include some of the more inflammatory descriptive characterizations made by government officials. It may be that their use results from the semantic difficulties caused by lack of nominal words with which to characterize perpetrators of political violence.

A striking facet of the data is that 94.3% of the characterizations (1,121 out of a total of 1,189) were media characterizations. These included headline characterizations and description, observation, and paraphrase in the articles. Only 3% of the characterizations were direct quotes of government officials, and 2% were direct quotes of witnesses.

This finding means that media quoted primary sources less than 6% of the time. That number is far below what would normally be considered good practice and may result because many of the stories were small or because media personnel could not reach public officials and witnesses or gain statements from them, or that they chose not to use statements when collected.

Appendix 2.1:
Characterizations Listed by Type

Nominal Characterizations

Abduction	Commandeer	Kidnapping
Abductor(s)	Commando(s)	Killer(s)
Action	Destroyed	Killing
Armed man(men)	Explosion	Occupation
Assailant	Fire	Paramilitary unit
Assassination	(to) Force	Theft
Attack	Group	Threat(en)
Attacker(s)	Gunman(men)	Seizure
Blast	Hijacker(s)	Shooting
Blew up/Blow up	Hijacking	Soldier
Bomber(s)	Hostage taking	Violence
Bombing	Kidnapper(s)	

Descriptive Characterizations

Ambush	Evil	Pirate(s)
Anti-Semite(ic)	Extremist(s)	Radical(s)
Armed Propaganda	Freedom Fighter(s)	Radical (adj.)
Unit	Guerrilla(s)	Rebel(s)
Atrocity	Heroically	Revolutionary(ies)
Barbaric	Insurgent(s)	Rightist(s)
Brutal	Leftist(s)	Right-wing
Coward(s)	Left-wing	Sabotage
Cowardly	Militant(s)	Saboteur(s)
Criminal(s)	Murder(s)	Slaying
Criminal act	Murderer(s)	Suicide-bombing
Dastardly	Nationalist(s)	Terrorist(s)
Despicable	Neo-Fascist(s)	Terrorism
Dissident(s)	Piracy	

3

U.S. Newsmagazines'
Labeling of Terrorists

BRIAN K. SIMMONS

The use of terrorism as a violent political strategy has been increasing steadily throughout the world during the past two decades (Alexander & Cline, 1982). As incidents of terrorism have risen, so has the interest of scholars who have attempted to understand the media's relation to terrorism. This is partially attributable to the fact that many have come to view terrorism as a form of communication (Schmid & de Graaf, 1982). Thus it is necessarily worthwhile to examine its communicative impacts. This is primarily done by investigating the manner in which the media report the terrorist's act. The building blocks of the media's coverage are the labels that are attached to the terrorist. Media labels that are positively perceived are beneficial to terrorists, whereas negative ones are detrimental (Crenshaw, 1983). Both terrorists and researchers have vested interests in determining which labels are positively and negatively perceived, and when each is used. In this analysis, the media become a battleground, as terrorists wage a campaign to cajole the media gatekeepers into adopting terminology that casts them in a favorable light. Hence, one can imagine this area of research as focusing on the media's communicative response to the terrorist's communicative act.

The purpose of this chapter is twofold: to determine what factual conditions precipitate the descriptive labeling of terrorists by newsmagazines, and to determine the perceived positive and negative connotations of these labels. Specifically, three hypotheses were tested:

- (H1) U.S. newsmagazines will label terrorists with a more negatively perceived term when their acts impact U.S. citizens.
- (H2) U.S. newsmagazines will label terrorists with a more negatively perceived term when their acts oppose U.S. foreign policy.
- (H3) There will be a significant positive correlation between the degree of carnage resulting from a terrorist act and the use of a negative label by U.S. newsmagazines.

These hypotheses sprang from a review of the pertinent literature, which now follows.

Review of Literature

The current research emphasis with respect to terrorism and the media addresses the quality of coverage that terrorists receive. Osgood, Suci, and Tannenbaum (1957) indicate that synonymous words carry vastly different connotations. This is especially true of the labels that we attach to political groups (Schlesinger, 1981). Research has shown that value judgments are often implicitly contained in the political label that one designates for an individual or group. O'Brien (1977) states that "the terms 'force' and 'violence' are again like 'terrorist' and 'freedom fighter' largely emotive propaganda terms: which term we use about a given act depends not on the degree of force or violence involved, but on a view of its justification" (p. 91). Schmid and de Graaf (1982) hold that "words carry emotive connotations, implying varying guilt attribution, and can serve to neutralize or justify (in-)human acts. If a source can bring a medium to adopt its language, it has already won an important psychological victory" (p. 88).

As terrorists seek to use the media as a propaganda tool (Hacker, 1976; Livingstone, 1982), the impact of the type of coverage becomes evident. Schmid and de Graaf (1982) report that "it goes without saying that the media can to some extent precondition the response of readers to terrorist news" (p. 80). Crenshaw (1983) agrees: "A free press is essential for communicating the terrorist appeal to wide audiences. The mode and tone of reporting can obviously influence the reception of the message" (p. 29). Research has also suggested that media coverage of terrorism can confer legitimacy upon terrorists

(Schmid & de Graaf, 1982). Those working in the field recognize that *terrorism* has come to have many meanings. "The very word has become a touchstone for postures and beliefs about the nature of man and society, and the relation of law, order, and justice" (Bell, 1977 p. 477). Livingstone (1982) found that the term is used in a generic sense as a form of shorthand by governments and the media.

Researchers have noted the wide range of connotations that the term *terrorism* has come to hold. Rubenstein (1987) claims that "to call an act of political violence terrorist is not merely to describe it but to judge it. Descriptively, terrorism suggests violent acts by individuals or small groups. Judgementally, it implies illegitimacy" (p. 17). The term also apparently implies disapproval. O'Brien (1977) states that:

> The words "terrorism" and "terrorist" are not terms of scientific classification. They are imprecise and emotive. We do not apply them to all acts of politically-motivated violence nor to all people who commit such crimes. We reserve their use for politically-motivated violence of which we disapprove. The words imply a judgement—sometimes a very complex judgement—about the political context in which those whom we decide to call terrorists operate, and above all, a judgement about the nature of the regime under which and against which they operate. (p. 91)

The choice of labeling a group "terrorist" carries with it strong political and moral implications. The reverse is also true. That is, other terms substituted for *terrorism* carry positive connotations. Rubenstein (1987) elaborates:

> Organized political violence involving the participation of large numbers of people is generally recognized as war or revolution, with combatants designated as "soldiers", "guerrillas", "commandos", or "freedom fighters." These terms imply that their activities reflect the will and advance the interests of some large social group. Individual violence is frequently associated with madness or crime. To call its practitioners "terrorists" implies that, like lunatics or criminals, they constitute an isolated minority rather than representing a mass constituency. (p. 17)

Because the various labels for terrorists carry political connotations, it is not surprising that scholars believe that the political motives of those who attach the label are responsible for the selection of a given label. Clutterbuck (1977) states that "one man's terrorist is another man's freedom fighter. Where the far right see the hidden hand of communism behind every guerrilla they dislike, the far left see the CIA in the same role" (p. 18). Because of this, others beside the terrorists have a vested interest in the labeling of terrorists. Schlesinger (1981) indicates that "the language used by the media in describing acts of political violence is of crucial importance in the eyes of state agencies" (p. 75). ⁄

The press, not being in the business of drawing fine distinctions between types of fighting forces, makes use of terms with both positive and negative political connotations. Netanyahu (1986) writes that "the term 'guerrillas' (irregular forces that confine their attacks to military targets) is used by the press interchangeably with 'terrorists' (who, whenever possible, attack civilians and non-combatants)" (p. 109). One of the problems with this practice is that it blurs the distinction between what is truly terrorism and what is not. As Laqueur (1977) puts it: "The indiscriminate use of such terms as 'left-wing' and 'right-wing' and the inclination to take political ideology at face value have made an understanding of issues involved so much more difficult" (p. 14).

The earliest empirical research into the media's labeling of terrorism was done by Epstein (1977). He conducted a content analysis of the coverage of political violence in Latin America during the period 1970-1971 in three major U.S. newspapers. The purpose was to examine specifically how the term *terrorism* was used. His results showed that the term was used on the average only 21% of the time. Most often the term was used to refer to forms of "left-wing extremism," such as political kidnappings, bombings, and assassinations by anti-government organizations. And, significantly, 62% of the time the three newspapers used the term to describe an event that could have been described using another term. In only one fifth of the cases did the term apply to cases of government violence.

The next serious research into the matter was conducted by Schmid and de Graaf (1982). They surveyed several international journalists and editors, asking them what kinds of political violence their medium commonly labeled as terrorism. They found that nine different actions were given the label of terrorism. In order of decreasing frequency they were: hijacking for coercive bargaining, bombing, assassination, hostage taking, guerrilla warfare, hijacking for escape, torture, kidnapping, and sabotage. Although revealing, the authors state that their sample size ($n = 27$) was too small to be of anything other than indicative value. Still, their work provides a glimpse into the mind-set of the mass media.

Weimann (1985) provided the first micro-investigation of the media's labeling of terrorism. The basic assumption of the study was that the content elements of the media's coverage should be considered. He hypothesized that "an inverse correlation existed between the geographical distance, political distance, and rate of violence of a political event and the positive evaluative loading of the label used in the press to describe the terrorists" (p. 435). His content analysis of 381 terrorist incidents in Israel's major newspapers from January 1979 to December 1981 revealed that the most effective factor in determining the use of a positive or negative label is political distance. In addition, it was found that a wide variety of labels was used to describe what his study defined as terrorism. Weimann's study is useful; however, it is limited somewhat by the fact that it was confined to Israel—a nation beset by domestic terrorism, with deep convictions on the subject. Unfortunately, its applicability to U.S. media is suspect.

A more recent study of the media's labeling of terrorism dealt with the characterizations of acts and the perpetrators of political violence in elite U.S. daily newspapers (see Picard & Adams, Chapter 2). Three elite newspapers were content-analyzed for their coverage of terrorist acts during the period 1980-85. The resulting characterizations were dichotomized into categories of nominal and descriptive. The study also classified the characterizations according to whether they were made by government officials, witnesses, or journalists. Picard and Adams found that "media personnel and witnesses to the violence tend to use nominal characterizations, and government officials tend to use descriptive characterizations." The study's results call into question the charges that the media are sensationalistic in their coverage of terrorism. Also noted was that over 94% of the characterizations were made by the media, suggesting that attribution is used infrequently in the coverage of terrorism. The major shortcoming of this research is that the categorization of terms as "nominal" or "descriptive" does not appear to have been done scientifically. If this is true, the categorization may be based upon unsupported assumptions.

The present study serves as a companion to Weimann's (1985) and Picard and Adam's work. Like the two previous studies, this one examines the labels that are given to the perpetrators of terrorist acts. Similar to the Weimann study, the present study seeks to match the factual setting of the act with the choice of label. Whereas the

Weimann study did so with the Israeli press (and Picard and Adams with elite U.S. daily newspapers), this study does so with weekly U.S. newsmagazines. The current study is also the first to factor in the variable of the involvement of U.S. citizens. In sum, this study fills a gap in the current research on the media's labeling of terrorists.

Methodology

The present study was conducted in two stages: a content analysis of newsmagazines, and the administration of a descriptive instrument tool that was completed by respondents. In the first stage, a systematic random sample of articles dealing with terrorism from *Time*, *Newsweek*, and *U.S. News & World Report* during the period from March 1980 through March 1988 were content analyzed. The total study population was 370, of which 185 articles were selected. Each article served as the unit of analysis, and the label attached to the perpetrator of a terrorist act served as the coding unit. The articles were also coded for the factual circumstances surrounding the act. The circumstances used as variables included the newsmagazine publishing the article, the descriptive label used, the type of terrorist act, the degree of carnage involved in the act, the political orientation of the terrorists, and whether U.S. citizens were involved in the act as victims. Each dependent variable was cross-tabulated with the independent variable (descriptive label) in order to yield a frequency count for each and an identification as to how the label use broke down according to dependent variables.

The second stage of the study, the descriptive instrument survey, was undertaken in order to ascertain the connotations of the labels used by the newsmagazines in describing the perpetrators of terrorist acts. A random sample of 120 college students at a medium-sized western university completed a survey made up of a semantic differential and an ordinal ranking scale. The semantic differential scale asked each respondent to rate each label according to six 7-point scales (good-bad, kind-cruel, valuable-worthless, fair-unfair, honest-dishonest, and brave-cowardly) that were selected because of their substantial evaluative loadings (Osgood, Suci, & Tannenbaum, 1957). The seven points of the scale were as follows: 3, 2, 1, 0, −1, −2, −3. The ordinal ranking scale asked respondents to rank order the thirteen labels used by the media to describe the perpetrators of terrorist acts.

These results were used as a cross-check on the findings of the semantic differential scale.

The data were first descriptively summarized. The mean score for each label, accumulated across the six semantic differential scales, was computed in order to arrive at the total evaluative load figure. The overall average for each label was then used to compare the labels. The range of responses was also computed. The ordinal ranking scale was summarized in an identical fashion. The data were analyzed using version 4.21 of the Number Cruncher Statistical System (NCSS). The level of significance was set at .05. To test H1 and H2, unpaired t-tests were conducted among all possible combinations of terms to determine whether certain terms that were similarly perceived could be grouped together. This resulted in grouping the terms into three categories: those labels perceived positively, somewhat negatively, and highly negatively. A chi-square analysis was then done in order to examine the relationship between the dependent variables with the three groups. To test H3, Pearson's product moment correlation (r) was computed and used to examine the relationship between the dependent variables and the three categories of variables. In interpreting Pearson's r, a scale suggested by Hinkle, Wiersma, and Jurs (1979) was used.

Results

Results will first be presented for the content analysis portion of the study. A total of 13 different labels were used by the three newsmagazines. The most commonly used term was *terrorist,* being used 65% of the time (120 uses, $n = 185$). The second most widely used label was *gunman,* which appeared 7% of the time (13 uses). The remaining labels (in order of frequency of use) were *guerrilla* (11 uses), *attacker* (9 uses), *extremist* (8 uses), *radical,* (8 uses), *hijacker* (6 uses), *revolutionary* (4 uses), *nationalist* (2 uses), *armed man* (1 use), *leftist* (1 use), *rightist* (1 use), and *militiaman* (1 use). It should be noted that the 13 labels observed were inclusive of the list that Picard and Adams (see Chapter 2) found in their study of elite U.S. daily newspapers.

With respect to the involvement of U.S. citizens in terrorist acts, it was found that U.S. citizens were involved in 91 of the 185 reported terrorist acts (49%). When U.S. citizens were involved, news-magazines chose to use the label *terrorist* to describe the perpetrators on nearly 80% of the occasions. However, when U.S. citizens were not involved, they used the term only 51% of the time. Interestingly, *terrorist, rightist,* and *hijacker* were the only labels to be used more frequently when U.S. citizens were involved than when they were not. *Hijacker* was used five times as often when U.S. citizens were involved. Only one term, *extremist,* was selected equally as often under both conditions (4 uses each).

With respect to the political orientation of terrorists, it was found that the only comparison that could be made was between those who opposed U.S. policy and those neutral toward it. This was because the third category (those favoring U.S. policy) had an unacceptably low number of observations (5) to be of any value. The findings revealed that those opposed to U.S. policy committed nearly twice as many terrorist acts as those classified as neutral (113 to 67). When those opposed to U.S. policy committed a terrorist act, newsmagazines labeled them as *terrorists* 72% of the time. However, the same term was used only 55% of the time when the act was committed by those neutral toward U.S. policy. Yet, the term *terrorist* still led the way among all labels for those neutral toward U.S. policy. In addition, the labels *gunman, leftist, rightist, revolutionary, hijacker,* and *extremist* were all used more frequently to describe those opposed to U.S. policy than to describe those neutral towards U.S. policy.

With respect to the degree of carnage, the label *terrorist* pervaded all categories of carnage. When no lives were lost, the term was used 73% of the time (41 of 55 observations). However, once the degree of carnage included the loss of lives, the use of the term dropped off. For example, when only 1 life was lost, the term was used 53% of the time; when 2 to 5 lives were lost the term was used 64% of the time; and when 6 to 11 lives were lost, the term was used 46% of the time. Only when 11 or more lives were lost did the frequency of use begin to approach that of acts where there were no lives lost. None of the 13 labels showed a linear increase or decrease in use as the categories changed. An interesting pattern of dispersion was also found. When there was no loss of life, the newsmagazines used nine terms. However, when there were two to five lives lost, 11 of the 13 labels were used. The remaining categories of carnage used only 6 of the 13 labels. Furthermore, four terms (*terrorist, guerrilla, gunman,* and *attacker*) were mentioned in each category.

The second stage of the study was a survey of 120 respondents to gauge the connotations of the labels. Nine of the terms were found to have a mean score signifying a negative perception. In order of negative perception, the terms were *hijacker, terrorist, attacker, gunman, guerrilla, leftist, armed-man, extremist,* and *radical.* The remaining terms were found to have a mean score signifying a positive connotation. These were (in order of positive perception) *nationalist, militiaman, revolutionary,* and *rightist.* Unpaired *t*-tests were conducted among all possible combinations of labels in order to determine perceived differences and similarities among terms. The *t*-tests allowed the terms to be grouped into three categories: highly negatively perceived (*terrorist, hijacker,* and *attacker*), somewhat negatively perceived (*guerrilla, radical, gunman, leftist, armed man, rightist,* and *extremist*), and somewhat positively perceived (*nationalist, revolutionary,* and *militiaman*). A final *t*-test was conducted among each of the three groups to determine whether each was perceived differently. The results of this test indicated that they were.

The results of the respective hypotheses are as follows:

- H1 (newsmagazines will label terrorists with a negative term when their acts involve U.S. citizens) was supported using the chi-square test ($\chi = 17.71$; df = 2/183; $p < .05$).

- H2 (newsmagazines will label terrorists with a negative term when their acts oppose or are neutral toward U.S. policy) was not supported using the chi square analysis ($\chi = 7.88$; df = 4/181; $p < .05$).

- H3 (there will be a positive correlation between the use of a negative label and the degree of carnage) was not supported using Pearson's product moment correlation ($r = .0071$).

Conclusions

This study was an attempt to determine what labels were used in the reporting of terrorist acts by U.S. newsmagazines, and how those labels were perceived. The conclusions drawn from these findings are presented according to each of the hypotheses, the relationship between type of act and label chosen, perceptions of labels, charges of media bias, and suggestions for further research.

The first hypothesis to be tested stated that newsmagazines would label terrorists with terms that were more negatively perceived when their acts impacted U.S. citizens. This hypothesis was supported. A chi-square analysis confirmed that the involvement of U.S. citizens was a strong influence on the newsmagazines' choice of label. These findings suggest that the media adopt a more negative interpretation toward terrorist acts when U.S. citizens are involved. The most negative term according to the ordinal ranking scale, *terrorist,* was used 79% of the time when U.S. citizens were involved in a terrorist incident, but only about half the time when they were not. Although the latter is still a high rate of use, the drop-off between categories is considerable. This drop-off was higher than that of all other labels. Another frequently used descriptive label when U.S. citizens were involved was *hijacker,* which was the most negative label according to the semantic differential scale. This term also showed an unusually high drop-off rate (67%) when compared with instances when U.S. citizens were not involved in a terrorist incident.

One interesting finding was that the word *attacker* was closely associated with the terms *terrorist* and *hijacker* in terms of similar negative perceptions. However, its frequency of use actually increased when U.S. citizens were not involved. One reason explaining this may be that the term *attacker* might be used in a more generic sense by the media, whereas *terrorist* and *hijacker* might be more restricted in their use to certain types of acts. This is supported by the fact that nearly one half of the term's uses in this study were found to be in incidents classified as attacks as opposed to, say, hijackings or bombings.

With the exception of the term *rightist,* the four terms with a net positive perception according to the semantic differential scale were all used more frequently when U.S. citizens were not involved than when they were. It must be noted that those four terms were, for the most part, perceived as being the same. Again, this supports the trend showing the newsmagazine's use of more negatively perceived terms when U.S. citizens are involved in terrorist acts.

It must be concluded that the media are greatly swayed by the involvement of U.S. citizens in terrorism. As it has been shown that the labeling of terrorists is often a judgmental act, it makes sense that the judgment is partially based on the degree to which the journalists and their readers can identify with those involved in the incident. This study indicates that such is the case, and, when U.S. citizens are involved in a terrorist act, the chances are very good that a negatively perceived label for terrorists will be used.

The second hypothesis to be tested stated that U.S. newsmagazines would label terrorists with terms that are more negatively perceived when their acts oppose U.S. policy. This hypothesis was not supported, as the variable was not found to have a statistically significant relationship to the news-magazines' choice of label. It is worth noting that two of the three most negatively perceived terms (*terrorist* and *hijacker*) were used more than twice as often when the terrorists opposed U.S. policy compared to when they were neutral toward it. However, this is merely indicative. What this means is that the charges which are often leveled against the media—that they label terrorists according to their political whims—are not true. In fact, to the extent that no statistically significant relationship was found, then it can be said that the newsmagazines are not sugarcoating terrorists in any way. This study found the media to be admirably fair in their treatment of those groups favoring, opposing, and neutral toward U.S. policy.

The third hypothesis to be tested stated that there would be a positive correlation between the degree of carnage resulting from a terrorist incident and the use of negatively perceived terms by U.S. newsmagazines. This hypothesis was not supported by the findings of this study. Pearson's product moment correlation indicated little if any positive correlation. All 13 of the descriptive labels showed a great deal of variation as the degree of carnage changed. The most negatively perceived term according to the ordinal ranking scale, *terrorist,* actually decreased in use from a frequency of 41 uses when no lives were lost to 25 uses when 11 or more lives were lost. Likewise, another negatively perceived term, *hijacker,* was found to follow a similar pattern of inverse correlation. The net result of these findings is that the media seem to be indifferent to the degree of carnage insofar as their choices of labels are concerned. Neither the positively perceived nor negatively perceived labels seemed to have a monopoly on any level of carnage. One could reasonably conclude that newsmagazines are quite consistent in their use of descriptive labels across the spectrum of violence.

It was not hypothesized that there would be a relationship between the type of act committed and the newsmagazines' use of a negatively perceived label. However, the results of the study suggest that the type of act is a statistically significant influence on the choice of label. The chi square statistic reveals that such a relationship exists. For example, when a killing was involved, the four most negatively perceived terms according to both instruments accounted for nearly

75% of all uses. Likewise, over 80% of the bombings carried a negatively perceived label, whereas all but one of the 16 incidents of hijacking resulted in the use of a negatively perceived label. During hostage-taking incidents, the newsmagazines chose a negatively perceived label over 73% of the time. The threat of a terrorist incident brought the use of a negatively perceived label nearly 95% of the time. This might mean that there is a sort of predisposition on the part of the media toward negative terms. Research into this area would be interesting.

One of the cornerstones of the study was the determination of which labels were positively and negatively perceived. Many terms were perceived as being similar. For example, *terrorist, hijacker,* and *attacker* have similar connotations. This suggests that there is a variety of terms at the media's disposal that can convey the same emotive message. Somewhat surprising is the inclusion of *attacker* in that list. Picard and Adams in Chapter 2 classify *attacker, gunman,* and *hijacker* as nominally descriptive terms. However, this stems from an arbitrary classification by the researchers, and is not empirically based. Thus it would appear that the terms have a different meaning than was previously assumed. It may well be that the media, in thinking they were selecting a positive or neutral term, were really selecting a negative one. This flies in the face of accusations that the media romanticize terrorists. In fact, it suggests that the opposite is true.

It also suggests that many of the descriptive labels are closely associated, forming groups of words with similar connotations. For example, the terms *extremist, rightist, leftist, radical,* and *armed man* are all seen as being virtually the same. This is true even though some of the terms had a net positive evaluative mean score whereas others did not. In fact, the terms *rightist* and *leftist* were perceived as being almost identical. Also, many of these terms may appear to be more inflammatory than they actually are. Picard and Adams classify them in Chapter 2 as descriptive terms. However, this study indicates that, although they may be descriptive, they are certainly equivalent in their connotations.

Third, few of the terms had a full range of responses. That is, many of the terms were seen by some respondents as being either completely positive or completely negative. For example, the term *militia-man* was the second most positively perceived term. However, its range was 36 points, meaning that it ranked by some as totally positive and by some as totally negative. In all, only two other terms showed the same result (*revolutionary* and *radical*). The average range for the remaining terms was 27.3 points, which was still a rather large range. Generally, the negative terms had a smaller range than did the positive ones, suggesting that their classification is somewhat safer. What can be accurately surmised is that the terms, although being extremely similar overall, can be perceived quite differently by certain people. That translates into a warning not to see studies such as this as definitive works on the perceptions of terms. Indeed, it may be that a different methodology is necessary in order to measure more accurately the meanings of these terms to respondents.

The present study grew out of a body of literature critical of the mass media's coverage of terrorism. In particular, it has been claimed that the incorrect choice of label for terrorists at once romanticizes them, grants them undue legitimacy, and contributes to the growth of their cause (e.g., O' Sullivan, 1986). Fortunately, the findings of this study do not in any way support such claims. First, there was no indication that the newsmagazines' choice of label could be construed as romanticizing terrorists. What was found was a consistent use of negatively perceived labels in a variety of situations. Unless these negatively perceived terms can be shown to be romantic, it must be concluded that the opposite is true. While this study does not purport to measure this per se, the results strongly suggest the rejection of such unfounded claims.

Second, it can be inferred fairly from the results that undue legitimacy was not granted by the newsmagazine's choice of label. Crenshaw (1983) in particular is critical of the media's tendency to legitimize terrorists unfairly, yet her writings are not based upon empirical research. To the contrary, the findings here reveal that the most commonly used label was that of *terrorist* (120 of 185 observed labels). Crenshaw and others call on the media to describe terrorists as they really are. It would seem they are doing so. The use of the word *terrorist* cut across all situations and spanned all variables. To the extent that it clearly dominated this study, it should be obvious that whatever legitimacy is being conferred is being done in negligible amounts. Again, the results of this study do not support such a conclusion per se, but it is strongly implied.

Third, it is unclear what relationship exists between the growth of terrorism and the media (see Picard in Chapter 5, and Eke & Alali in Chapter 1), to the extent that it is hard to accept claims that qualitative media coverage of terrorism is a contributing factor in the growth of certain terrorist movements. Granted, this study does not attempt to answer such questions. However, when one considers the frequency with which negatively perceived labels were used, it is clear that this might in some way mitigate against claims of a causal relationship between the two. Tuchman (1978), Gitlin (1980), and Altheide (1976) all suggest that ideology is conveyed by mass media messages. Their work also indicates that negative perceptions might deter the acceptance of a given ideology under certain conditions. Hence, this study at least casts doubt as to the validity of allegations linking the mass media's coverage of terrorism to the spread of the phenomenon.

Finally, this chapter has given empirical answers to many of the questions and charges leveled against the media. Much literature concerning the mass media's coverage of terrorism is speculative in nature. Often, sweeping statements are made without any substantive proof. This chapter has shown through social science research that the charges leveled against the media can be answered by careful research. It was alleged that the media labeled terrorists as anything but terrorists. The present study revealed that *terrorist* was the overwhelming choice of U.S. newsmagazines when labeling terrorists. It was alleged that the media presented terrorists in a favorable light by using positively perceived terms to describe them. This study found that the words used are perceived so similarly that there could not be that great of a difference among many of them; it was also found that the most negatively perceived terms were also the most frequently used. It was alleged that the political nature of the perpetrators of terrorist acts determined the label they received. The present study revealed that in reality no such statistically significant relationship exists. Thus one can conclude that this study helps dispel many false notions as to the nature and effects of the media's coverage of terrorism.

There are many opportunities for further research into this area. Three will briefly be outlined here. First, a hypothesis might be constructed that proposes a positive correlation between a certain type of terrorist act and the label that would be used to describe its perpetrators. Indeed, such an investigation would certainly be warranted in light of the findings of this study. It might help reconcile what could be two competing factors influencing the newsmagazines' choice of labels. It has been proven that the involvement of U.S. citizens bears greatly on the choice of label. However, if the type of act is also a factor, further research would be in order to determine the strengths of the two influences upon each other. Also, further research into the specifics of the act as compared to the descriptive label chosen might also be fruitful. For the purposes of this study, broad classifications were made in terms of the types of acts committed. A future study might more closely examine the intricate nature of specific acts in order to ascertain their impact on the labels that were chosen.

Second, work needs to be done comparing the newsmagazines' choices of labels to those of other media. The bulk of the literature arguably condemns all media coverage of terrorism. However, television in particular seems to bear the brunt of the criticism. Although the present study clears newsmagazines to some extent, the same may not be true of other media. Television needs to be examined for factors affecting choice of label. One might suspect that the present results could be applied to television as well. However, this may not be the case, and it is certainly worthwhile to investigate. Of special interest might be the labeling of terrorists by correspondents as opposed to anchors, and so forth. Another idea might be a longitudinal study examining the labeling of a terrorist group over time.

Finally, further research is needed to determine the extent to which descriptive labels confer legitimacy upon terrorist groups. One potential study might entail a survey to ascertain a label's perceived representation of legitimacy. Alternatively, one might undertake a case study investigating the labeling of a fairly mature, legitimized group like the PLO. Any work that might link the process of accepting a group or cause with the media's coverage of terrorism would be beneficial.

Certainly the present study has its limitations. Only the three largest weekly newsmagazines were examined. Further research might widen the population of magazines. The study was completed with a fairly low number of respondents ($n = 120$) to the descriptive instrument survey. The next generation of research might want to include a larger response group. And future researchers might want to undertake a factor analysis of the data in order to determine more confidently the relationships between variables. However, the present study is useful in determining the reality of terrorist labeling and the myths surrounding it.

Finally, it must be noted that the study drew inferences about mass media sources based upon the perceptions of the receivers of their messages. Clearly, such hypothesizing is a risky proposition. Although appropriate safeguards were implemented in this study to allow such generalizations to be made, further research that more directly speaks to this question is necessary. For example, the next generation of research might have the writers of U.S. newsmagazine articles actually respond to the survey instruments. In this manner, the conceptual leap from receivers back to sources would not be as large. However, such generalizations are made every day. Specific to this study, those who responded to this study were the readers of the three newsmagazines. In this sense, the conceptual leap is not as large. The best research will see to it that every precaution is taken to assure its internal validity. As it now stands, the current study adds a great deal to the present understanding of the media's labeling of terrorists.

References

Alexander, Y., & Cline, R. S. (1982). Worldwide chronology of terrorism: 1981. *Terrorism, 6,* 107-388.

Altheide, D. (1976). *Creating reality: How TV news distorts events.* Beverly Hills, CA: Sage.

Bell, J. B. (1977). Trends of terror: The analysis of political terror. *World Politics, 19,* 476-488.

Clutterbuck, R. (1977). *Guerrillas and terrorists.* Athens: Ohio University Press.

Crenshaw, M. (Ed.). (1983). *Terrorism, legitimacy, and power.* Middletown, CT: Wesleyan University Press.

Epstein, E. C. (1977). The uses of terrorism. *Stanford Journal of International Studies, 12,* 68-71.

Gitlin, T. (1980). *The whole world is watching.* Berkeley: University of California Press.

Hacker, F. (1976). *Crusaders, criminals, and crazies: Terror and terrorism in our time.* New York: Norton.

Hinkle, D., Weirsma, W., & Jurs, S. (1979). *Applied statistics for the behavioral sciences.* Chicago: Rand McNally.

Laqueur, W. (1977). *Terrorism: A study of national and international political violence.* New York: New American.

Livingstone, N. C. (1982). *The war against terrorism.* Lexington, MA: Lexington.

Netanyahu, B. (Ed.). (1986). *Terrorism: How the West can win.* New York: Farrar, Strauss, and Giroux.

O'Brien, C. C. (1977). Liberty and terrorism. *International Security, 2,* 56-57.

Osgood, C., Suci, G., & Tannenbaum, P. (1957). *The measurement of meaning*. Urbana: University of Illinois Press.

O'Sullivan, J. (1986). Deny them publicity. In Netanyahu, B. (Ed.), *Terrorism: How the West can win*. New York: Farrar, Strauss, and Giroux.

Rubenstein, R. (1987). *Alchemists of revolution: Terrorism in the modern world*. New York: Basic Books.

Schlesinger, P. (1981). Terrorism, the media, and the liberal-democratic state: A critique of orthodoxy. *Social Research, 42*, 74-99.

Schmid, A., & de Graaf, J. (1982). *Violence as communication*. Beverly Hills: Sage.

Tuchman, G. (1978). *Making news: A study in the construction of reality*. New York: Free Press.

Weimann, G. (1985). Terrorists or freedom fighters? Labeling terrorism in the Israeli press. *Political Communication and Persuasion, 2*, 433-445.

4

The Journalist's Role in
Coverage of Terrorist Events

ROBERT G. PICARD

Although journalists consider themselves dispassionate recorders of terrorist events, conveying objective and factual information about incidents, their roles in such events are seen quite differently by authorities, media critics, and scholars. These differences in views result because journalists have traditionally employed four rhetorical traditions in conveying news, and these affect the meaning received by audiences.

The first is the information tradition, which emphasizes factual information and documentation of events. When this is employed, a calm, dispassionate conveyance of information occurs. Such "raw journalism" is often found in initial news reports of terrorist events. The second tradition, sensationalism, is emotional. Material is presented in ways that emphasize alarm, threat, provocation, anger, and fear. This type of presentation, which is used in a variety of types of reporting, works well in the reporting of conflict and terrorism because the subject is likely to bring an emotional response and contains inherently dramatic and tragic elements that can be sensationally reported. The third journalistic tradition of storytelling is that of the feature story, which contains significant symbolism and often focuses on individuals as heroes or villains, victims or perpetrators. This type of story focuses on individuals to provide a context that helps to put news events and larger issues into a personal perspective. In the reporting of terrorism, this can take the form of stories about what it was like to be a hostage or what it is like to live in a repressive nation

40

Table 4.1 Sample Leads for News Stories Using Different Rhetorical
Traditions

Information Tradition

"Four persons were killed and 33 others injured when a bomb exploded in a café in downtown Paris Thursday."

Sensationalist Tradition

"A terrorist bomb ripped a crowded Paris cafe Thursday, mortally wounding four persons and leaving 33 persons covered with blood from their injuries."

Feature Story Tradition

"A couple on their honeymoon was killed Thursday when a bomb destroyed a Paris café. The bride and groom, who had been married for less than 24 hours, were among 4 persons killed and 33 wounded when the bomb exploded."

Didactic Tradition

"The bombing of a Paris café Thursday is believed to signal a new wave of violence by Moslem fundamentalists angered by French foreign policy in the Middle East."

---

in which individuals are striking out at the government. The fourth tradition, the didactic approach, stresses explanation and education about how and why things work. Articles about the tactics of terrorists or authorities often fall into this category.

Which of these traditions is utilized helps to determine the meaning conveyed about the events. A dispassionate approach will result in a less emotional response or lessened fear on the part of the reader or viewer. A sensationalistic approach can increase fear and, not incidentally, improve newspaper sales and television viewership. An approach emphasizing violence and threat might make the news appear more significant than an approach that downplays such violence. A news report about any incident can be constructed by employing any of the traditions (see Table 4.1). Which tradition is selected depends upon the reporter and editors involved.

When the information tradition is employed, the accuracy of description of overt occurrences is generally high. Government officials, for instance, rely heavily on journalistic accounts of events and often take as long as 36 to 48 hours to get response teams in place that can collect their own information when incidents take place in other nations.

Terrorist acts are not merely random events, however. Most incidents of terrorism are symbolic, with meaning assigned to them by those who perpetrate the acts, as well as by officials, victims, and journalists. Thus the kind of reporting, the techniques used, and the messages conveyed in the news are crucial in helping form the meaning assigned to acts by media audiences.

Journalistic emphasis on descriptions of what is visible, however, can easily create distortions and confusion in the meaning that is constructed by audiences because most of what occurs in terrorist events is invisible to journalists; they must rely upon information and statements from authorities about the events. Victims and their friends and relatives are sometimes available, but their knowledge of events is generally limited to the overt violence and its aftermath.

Because of the inability to explore events significantly and dependence upon official sources, much terrorism coverage involves significant struggles for rhetorical control (Crelinsten, 1987; Gerbner, 1988). Journalists play a variety of roles in this persuasive atmosphere and are deeply involved in the construction of rhetorical visions about terrorism and its perpetrators. Journalists amplify, arbitrate, and create their own rhetoric about terrorist acts.

Journalists as Rhetorical Amplifiers

In this role, journalists gain the attention of audiences and convey messages about political violence by providing the platform and amplification system by which this can be accomplished.

Dowling (1988a, pp. 18-19) argues that this amplification is important because a primary rhetorical message of terrorists is to gain the attention of and convey their existence to the public. Thus violent events are created in order to gain coverage that will convey this message to audiences.

Another objective of some terrorists is to gain forums in which to air their grievances and ideas, a goal often separated from specific violence. Because media organizations are institutions that support and perpetuate the basic norms and values of the dominant order, such access is rarely provided to those groups at the fringes of society. Because terrorists do not operate within the acceptable parameters of normal society, their views are rarely conveyed within media. By engaging in violence, terrorists hope to force journalists to attend to their views, and to expose and explain their beliefs (Picard, 1986). This is why many perpetrators of political violence issue statements to be published and broadcast and are willing to grant interviews to reporters.

Weimann (1983) has shown media coverage to be beneficial to terrorists by increasing awareness of their existence and "recognition of the political, racial, or religious problem that caused the event" (p. 44). This benefit is not widely available, however, because journalists only rarely amplify messages about the situational causes of such violence (see Atwater in Chapter 6; Decker & Rainey, 1982; Milburn, Bowley, Fay-Dumaine, & Kennedy, 1987; Paletz, Ayanian, & Fozzard, 1982b) unless lengthy, ongoing terrorist events are reported (Picard, 1987) or specialty media—those not intended for mass, general audiences—are involved (Fuller, 1988).

Journalists also amplify the rhetoric of government officials and leaders of other institutions targeted in or responding to political violence. The primary goals of such rhetoric are to show society's strength and stability, to marginalize perpetrators, and to gain support for public policies. The primary means by which these goals are supported is through the official rhetoric that defines and explains terrorist incidents and their significance as conveyed during news conferences, interviews with reporters, and appearances on news and talk shows. Journalists, who are highly dependent on official sources for information and statements, thus amplify officials' rhetoric that creates a perceptual reality for the audience. Government views and reactions thus become a major focus of news coverage of terrorist events, and officials and former officials are the main sources of information and comment (see Atwater in Chapter 6; Atwater & Green, 1988; Paletz, Ayanian, & Fozzard, 1982a, 1982b; Picard, 1987).

Journalists as Arbitrators of Rhetoric

Because journalists rely heavily on easily identifiable news values in making decisions about whether to cover events, media organizations are vulnerable to manipulation by terrorists and interested parties, including government officials and supporters of terrorism (Picard, 1989). In such situations journalists attempt to arbitrate the rhetoric of perpetrators and interested parties with their own agendas so that the ability to manipulate coverage does not alter the meaning of events in such ways that reality is distorted. Unfortunately, journalists' success in doing so is often limited.

Evidence of arbitration is seen in comparisons of how media personnel describe terrorist events and their perpetrators and how government officials make similar descriptions. Picard and Adams (see Chapter 2) found that media and witnesses tended to use more neutral or straightforward words and terms in descriptions, whereas government officials used inflammatory and judgmental words and terms. Thus what journalists and witnesses might describe as an "explosion," officials would label a "despicable attack by those with no regard for life."

The difficulty of arbitrating authorities' rhetoric is compounded because journalists rarely have direct entry to the site of the events and because access to participants in incidents is rare. The perpetrators of terrorism are almost always unavailable for comment and the security and policy officials directly involved rarely make themselves available to journalists.

The inability of journalists to make contact with individuals with first-hand knowledge and participation in events thus forces journalists to seek substitutes. These substitutes are typically elected or appointed political officials who have little knowledge about the incident, but rather have specific policy agendas relating to terrorism or the conflicts related to the violence. Journalists also seek out security experts for comment, but those who are available generally do not have specific knowledge of the event or often do not know who perpetrated it. In many cases, the specialists are former government security or political officials who are also guided by policy agendas.

Cooper (1988) has argued that journalists covering terrorist incidents with international aspects do so with adversarial perspectivism that affects how they view incidents and explanations of incidents. These factors thus make it impossible for journalists to report such events objectively outside of the perspective of their national interests. Such factors result in unequal arbitration of the rhetoric of the political violence and authorities that ultimately favors the status quo.

Journalists as Creators of Rhetoric

It was noted above that journalists create rhetoric whenever they report terrorist events and that the rhetorical tradition employed determines the nature of the rhetoric. Also important is the role of formats, that is, presentation conventions that are used to package information and that determine the significance and the types of information that news packages carry. Elements of such formats are the focus of the report, the sources of information, and the actual means by which these and other elements are presented.

Print and broadcast formats diverge when it comes to the means by which information is packaged for delivery to audiences because of the inherent differences in the media of delivery. Spatial and temporal elements of the two media differ significantly; these influence how information is provided and thus the structure and amount of information delivered. Television utilizes video and live representations that are unavailable to print media and thus can convey information with more immediacy and urgency.

On television, several types of packaging formats are typically used to deal with terrorist incidents: news bulletins, newsbreaks, newscasts, newsmagazines, current-affairs talk shows, and documentaries. Each has its own conventions for use of materials. Format differences also exist in newspaper coverage; presentation formats include news briefs, shorts, first-day stories, second-day and follow-up stories, news features, and interviews.

The dominant portrayals of terrorism on television come in the forms of news bulletins, newsbreaks, and newscasts, and most newspaper reports are briefs, shorts, and first-day reports. In both media, audiences receive short, staccato presentations that provide little contextual information and emphasize dramatic elements of conflict, threat, and casualties.

Formats selected for news reports about terrorism produce significantly different types of messages and meaning. News reports focus on events and tactics, whereas documentaries and interviews focus on causes and purposes. Altheide (1986) has shown that because few opportunities are presented for the latter type of format, journalists exercise significant control over information and its meaning.

The emphasis on short news reports thus creates significant misunderstanding about events and issues. Larson (1986) has argued that news coverage of Iran before the fall of the Shah, which consisted mainly of short news items, did not deal with political opposition in any systematic way and denigrated its importance. As a result, audiences received a mistaken view of the strength of the opposition, and the collapse of the government surprised many.

Developments that surrounded the formation of the new Iranian government and the seizure of the U.S. embassy were also reported in a way that distorted the meaning of the events and kept the public from understanding that a religious rather than merely a political revolution was underway.

Several studies also reveal that the themes and issues addressed in coverage of terrorism cast meanings upon news that have effects upon the perceptions of audiences. Palmerton (1985, 1988) argues that reporters covering the embassy seizure focused extensively on the policies and actions of the U.S. government, conveyed the meaning that U.S. government actions helped cause the seizure to take place, suggested that military intervention would reestablish control, and ultimately projected an image of powerlessness that the Iranians were able to exploit. Nevertheless, it appears that journalists did not depart significantly from official views and policy in dealing with the incident. Altheide (1981) has argued that both the content and style of television coverage supported administration policy during the event and that reporters acted as intermediaries between the U.S. government, the Iranian government, and the militants holding the embassy personnel hostage.

The images of the U.S. president and the leaders of Iran created by media rhetoric were examined by Dowling (1984), who found that journalists portrayed the Iranians as opportunistic or irrational, but that they differed in their presentations of President Carter. Some journalists portrayed him as strong, good, and restrained, whereas others portrayed him as weak, selfish, and ineffective.

Lule (1988) studied media rhetoric about victims of terrorism and found that journalists provided rhetorical visions that portrayed the victims as symbolic sacrifices in a manner that provoked intense identification with the victims by audiences.

Summary

Much of the research on media coverage of terrorism has focused on what is covered, how it is covered, how extensively it is covered, and other such issues that provide a descriptive and exploratory base for understanding coverage. More important, however, is the meaning of the messages conveyed. Journalists' roles in coverage of terrorism help the public develop perceptions about the world around them and influence the ways in which audiences relate to actors in terrorism.

The difficulties caused by the roles of journalists result from the selective use of labels and the word "terrorism" to identify acts and perpetrators and from the traditions and formats used in constructing news reports about incidents.

The effects of these roles are beginning to receive appropriate scrutiny, as evidenced by the growing body of studies emphasizing the results of the social dramas. Journalists, obviously, must be made sensitive to the power of what they report, but when dealing with the volatile area of reporting on terrorism, they must be especially sensitive to *how* they report the news as well.

Although many journalists are now concerned about the effects of their coverage on the outcomes of specific incidents of political violence and its effects on perpetrators and authorities, most journalists are unaware of or less concerned with the effects of their roles on the public because of the broader perceptions created by coverage. I would like to believe this lack of concern will diminish as scholars continue to address the social and political effects of the coverage and continue to explore and reveal its importance.

References

Altheide, D. L. (1981). Iran vs. U.S. TV news: The hostage story out of context. In William C. Adams (Ed.), *Television coverage of the Middle East* (pp. 128-158). Norwood, NJ: Ablex.

Altheide, D. L. (1986, April). *Format and symbols in TV coverage of terrorism in the United States and Great Britain.* Paper presented to the Pacific Sociological Association, Denver, CO.

Atwater, T., & Green, N. F. (1988). News sources in network coverage of international terrorism. *Journalism Quarterly 65*, 967-971.

Cooper, T. W. (1988). Terrorism and perspectivist philosophy: Understanding adversarial news coverage. *Terrorism and the News Media Research Project Monograph Series.*

Crelinsten, R. D. (1987). Power and meaning: Terrorism as a struggle of access to the communication structure. In P. Wilkinson (Ed.), *Contemporary research on terrorism.* Aberdeen, Scotland: Aberdeen University Press.

Decker, W., & Rainey, D. (1982, November). *Media and terrorism: Toward the development of an instrument to explicate their relationship.* Paper presented to the Speech Communication Association, Louisville, KY.

Dowling, R. E. (1984). *Rhetorical vision and print journalism: Reporting the Iran hostage crisis to America.* Doctoral dissertation, University of Denver.

Dowling, R. E. (1988a, March). *The contributions of speech communication scholarship to the study of terrorism and the news media: Preview and review.* Paper presented to the Communication in Terrorist Events Conference, Terrorism and the News Media Research Project, Boston.

Dowling, R. E. (1988b, September). *The terrorist and the media: Partners in crime or rituals and harmless observers.* Paper presented to the Media and Modern Warfare Conference, Centre for Conflict Studies, University of New Brunswick.

Fuller, L. K. (1988). Terrorism as treated by the *Christian Science Monitor*, 1977-1988. *Political Communication and Persuasion, 5* 121-138.

Gerbner, G. (1988). Symbolic functions of violence and terror. *Terrorism and the News Media Research Project Monograph Series.*

Larson, J. F. (1986). Television and U.S. foreign policy: The case of the Iran hostage crisis. *Journal of Communication, 36*, 108-127.

Lule, J. (1988, March). *Sacrifice, scapegoat, and the body on the tarmac: A terrorist victim in the New York Times.* Paper presented to the Communication in Terrorist Events Conference, Terrorism and the News Media Research Project, Boston.

Milburn, M. A., Bowley, C., Fay-Dumaine, J., & Kennedy, D. (1987, July). *Attributional analysis of the mass media coverage of terrorism.* Paper presented to the International Society for Political Psychology, San Francisco.

Paletz, D. L., Ayanian, J. Z., & Fozzard, P. A. (1982a, Spring). The IRA, the Red Brigades, and the FALN in the *New York Times. Journal of Communication, 32*, 162-172.

Paletz, D. L., Ayanian, J. Z., & Fozzard, P. A. (1982b). Terrorism on TV news: The IRA, the FALN, and the Red Brigades. In W. C. Adams (Ed.), *Television coverage of international affairs* (pp. 143-165). Norwood, NJ: Ablex.

Palmerton, P. R. (1985). *Terrorism and institutional targets as portrayed by news providers.* Paper presented to the Speech Communication Association.

Palmerton, P. R. (1988, Spring). The rhetoric of terrorism and media response to the "Crisis in Iran." *Western Journal of Speech Communication, 52*, 105-121.

Picard, R. G. (1986, Fall). The conundrum of news coverage of terrorism. *Toledo Law Review, 18*, 141-150.

Picard, R. G. (1987). Stages in coverage of incidents of political violence. *Terrorism and the News Media Research Project Paper Series* (No. 10).

Picard, R. G. (1989, September). *Terrorism and media values: News selection and the distortion of reality.* Paper presented to the Ethics and Foreign Policy Lecture Series, University of Connecticut at Hartford.

Weimann, G. (1983, Winter). The theater of terror: Effects of press coverage. *Journal of Communication, 33*, 38-45.

5

News Coverage as the Contagion of Terrorism

Dangerous Charges Backed by Dubious Science

ROBERT G. PICARD

When NBC News broadcast a three-and-a-half minute interview in May 1986 with Abul (Mohammed) Abbas, head of the Palestine Liberation Front which hijacked the *Achille Lauro* in 1985, the news organization was subjected to swift and pointed criticism. "Terrorism thrives on this kind of publicity," charged State Department spokesman Charles Redman. He said it "encourages the terrorist activities we're all seeking to deter" (Boyer, 1986, p. A7).

A similar response was seen in Great Britain when the British government attacked the BBC for its plans to broadcast the documentary "Real Lives: At the Edge of the Union," which included an interview with Martin McGuinness, a spokesman for the legal political wing of the Irish Republican Army who is accused of being a top-ranking official in the outlawed paramilitary group. Home Secretary Leon Britain asked the BBC not to air the program, saying it was "wholly contrary to the public interest" (Bellmann, 1986, p. 20).

AUTHOR'S NOTE: Reprinted with permission from *Political Communication and Persuasion*, Vol. 3 (Fall, 1986).

Such incidents have led to calls for more control over what is broadcast and printed about terrorism and those who engage in such political violence. At the American Bar Association meeting in London in 1985, Prime Minister Margaret Thatcher told the gathered attorneys that democracies "must find ways to starve the terrorists and hijackers of the oxygen of publicity on which they depend" (*New York Times*, 1985, p. A3). Her statement met with support from U.S. Attorney General Edwin Meese and other U.S. officials.

While these efforts have been aimed at getting media to adhere to voluntary guidelines, other individuals have suggested that legal restraints be imposed. Imposition of such restraints would face greater difficulty in the United States than abroad, because of the First Amendment, but many argue they are necessary to control terrorism and protect public safety.

Behind the efforts to induce self-restraints or impose government restraints on the media is the belief that coverage of terrorism and terrorists creates more terrorism and terrorists. The idea that media are the contagion of terrorism has been widely heralded and is repeatedly used to justify efforts to alter media coverage. This has occurred despite the fact that there is no significant evidence that media act as a contagion.

This chapter will review the argument that media coverage spreads terrorism by giving encouragement to those who engage in such violence and explore the literature upon which it is based. It will also suggest paradigms within which to view and explore media effects on terrorists that offer a variety of important research opportunities.

The Contagion Literature

During the past two decades the literature associating media with terrorism and implicating media as a contagion of such violence has grown rapidly. When carefully dissecting that literature, however, one finds that it contains no credible evidence that media are an important factor in inducing and diffusing terrorist acts.

Most books, articles, essays, and speeches on the topic consist of sweeping generalities, conjecture, supposition, anecdotal evidence based on dubious correlations, and endless repetition of equally weak arguments and nonscientific evidence offered by other writers on the subject of terrorism.

As one reviews the literature it becomes shockingly clear that not a single study based on accepted social science research methods has established a cause-effect relationship between media coverage and the spread of terrorism. Yet public officials, scholars, editors, reporters, and columnists continually link the two elements and present their relationship as proven.

The dearth of evidence associating the two variables is not the result of conflicting studies or arguments over interpretation of evidence, but rather the inexplicable absence of research on the subject. At times some scholars have attempted to overcome that problem or to place the pallor of respectability over their opinions by "borrowing" conclusions from the literature of the effects of televised violence and crime on viewers and then projecting similar effects to coverage of terrorism.

The use of this questionable tactic is disquieting to anyone who subscribes to social science research philosophy. It is especially disturbing when one considers the potential abrogation of civil liberties that could result and the unsettled state of knowledge about the effects of televised violence and crime.

Without wishing to cast aspersions on media violence research, it is safe to say that, in aggregate, the thousands of studies on the subject are contradictory, inconclusive, and based on widely differing definitions, methods, and assumptions. The literature has been the subject of some of the most heated debates in the social sciences.

Social learning, arousal, and disinhibition theories on the effects of media portrayals of violence and crime have nevertheless been transferred to the issue of terrorism portrayal. The results of studies supporting the views of terrorism researchers have been accepted in the face of conflicting evidence.

This has occurred despite the fact that studies on the effects of portrayals of violence and crime have yielded no cause-effect relationship. At best, it can be said that media portrayals do not cause the audience to become violent but may affect some media users who have antisocial tendencies and spread uncertainty and fear among others.

Although these violence research findings suggest reasonable hypotheses for terrorism research, no research along those lines has been conducted. Instead, what should only be hypotheses about media and terrorism have been accepted as fact.

Among the elements of the more fascinating pseudoscientific evidence offered in support of the notion that media are the contagion, reported in some of the most important sources on media and terrorism, are public opinion polls of political and law enforcement officials, as well as members of the public, about the relationship between media and terrorism. Although the polls present interesting insights into the perceptions of these individuals at given times, and add something to the understanding of how terrorism affects people, they are used by some writers as evidence that media are indeed the contagion of terrorism. Because the public and officials believe them to be the contagion, media must be the culprit, we are told.

Because the opinions of these groups of people are presumably affected by the agenda set by past statements of government officials, media critics, and terrorism control researchers—all of whom have repeatedly alleged the link between media and terrorism—it is not surprising that other officials and the public should parrot their views.

Despite such problems, the contagion argument is continually used against the media. Rudolf Levy (1985), a Defense Department expert on terrorism who has taught at the U.S. Army Intelligence Center and School, conveyed the media-as-contagion view throughout the military community in the publication *Military Intelligence*, saying:

> Experts believe that this type of coverage often has adverse effects, such as:
>
> - Encouraging the formation of new groups. Tactical successes and successful exploitation of the media lead to terrorists taking advantage of the momentum of previous actions and, thus, to an increase in terrorist acts.
> - Keeping the terrorist organization's name before the public and "the masses" on whose behalf the terrorists supposedly act.
> - Leading other less successful groups or individuals to commit more daring acts of terrorist violence.
> - Tempting terrorists, who have received favorable media coverage in the past, to attempt to seize control of the media. (p. 35)

A similar view has been expressed by the American Legal Foundation, a right-wing group that urged the government to restrict media coverage. The group argues that "because they give the terrorists a convenient state to vent their political grievances, the media actually encourage terrorism and may promote the increasing violence and drama of terrorist attacks" (American Legal Foundation, n. d., p. 24).

Some of the most recognizable names in terrorism research are less sanguine about the accuracy of the contagion hypothesis, but they have nevertheless embraced and/or diffused it widely. For example, M. Cherif Bassiouni (1983), who has written widely on the subject and taught many who are carrying on research and activities aimed at preventing or controlling political violence through legal means, recognizes the problems with the contagion idea but nevertheless does not reject it: "Although this hypothesis would not appear entirely susceptible to empirical verification, at least with respect to ideologically motivated individuals, concern over this contagion effect has been repeatedly expressed, and the theory retains a certain intuitive reasonableness" (p. 184). Other experts, such as Alex Schmid and Janny de Graaf (1982) at the Centre for the Study of Social Conflicts in the Netherlands, are willing to accept the contagion effect despite the lack of empirical evidence that it exists or that it would not exist if the media coverage were removed. Although admitting gaps in knowledge about the contagion effect they still argue:

> The most serious effect of media reporting on insurgent terrorism, however, is the likely increase in terroristic activities. The media can provide the potential terrorist with all the ingredients that are necessary to engage in this type of violence. They can reduce inhibitions against the use of violence, they can offer models and know-how to potential terrorists and they can motivate them in various ways. (p. 142)

Robert L. Rabe (1977), assistant chief of police for the Metropolitan Police Department in Washington, DC, also promoted the view that there may be value in the hypotheses. In his address at a terrorism conference, he stated:

> And what of the contagion of such detailed coverage of a terrorist incident? By glorifying terrorist activities with extensive news coverage, the event is projected as an attraction for others to emulate. If such is the case, terrorism has truly made the television media a pawn in the great game of propaganda. (p. 69)

Even members of the media have accepted the contagion idea. NBC News President Larry Grossman (1986) presented this view in a more popular form to a Society of Professional Journalists' meeting: "Does television allow itself to be 'used' by terrorists and does television coverage, therefore, encourage terrorist acts? The answer is yes to both. . . . The very existence of television undoubtedly bears some responsibility for the 'copycat' syndrome of terrorism today" (p. 38).

But not all terrorism scholars fully embrace the view. Brian Jenkins, director of the Rand Corporation's terrorism research, has argued that the media cannot be solely blamed for the spread of terrorism. "The news media are responsible for terrorism to about the same extent that commercial aviation is responsible for airline hijackings," he says. "The vast communications network that makes up the news media is simply another vulnerability in a technologically advanced and free society" (quoted in Schmid & de Graaf, 1982, p. 143).

Although there has never been a scientifically based study on the contagion effect of media coverage per se, several related contagion studies have been conducted and are of interest. The most significant study has been conducted by Midlarsky, Crenshaw, and Yoshida (1980), who sought to answer the question of why terroristic acts spread across nations in Western Europe and Latin America. Using the theory of hierarchy, the authors attempt to explain the spread of terrorism among the nations. In the case of Western Europe the authors found that "terrorism spread from the least powerful to the most powerful, from the weak states to the strong" (p. 276).

The Midlarsky study found that European terrorist groups, for example, borrowed ideology, rhetoric, and methods from the Third World. The biggest contagion effect was found in the transfers of the technique of bombing in both Latin America and Europe, with kidnappings most significant in Latin America and hijacking to a lesser extent there. Media were never mentioned as a cause of the diffusion of terrorist techniques.

Security adviser Edward Heyman and CIA researcher Edward Mickolus (1980, pp. 299-305) later disputed the full findings of the Midlarsky study, citing inadequacies in its data base and some of its inferences, but they did not dispute its general concept. The two argued that their own research indicated that two noncontagion diffusion factors were important in the spread of violence: extensive inter-group cooperation and the idea of transporting terrorist acts to locations where they could best be carried out. They argued that transportation was the biggest factor. Again, no mention of media coverage was made as being an important cause of the spread of terrorism.

Rand Corporation studies have found some evidence of contagion in the diffusion process of terrorist activity types. Jenkins (1981), although unwilling to completely damn news coverage as the culprit, has noted clusters of occurrences in airline hijackings and embassy sieges and indicated that media might have played a role in those occurrences. The inference, however, is based on no scientific evidence.

Other research on terrorism has noted that in the case of many airline hijackings in the 1970s, for example, terrorist hijackers often had specific knowledge of radio, navigation, and operating equipment on aircraft and of commercial aviation practices, suggesting they had specialized training and that extensive planning of campaigns of hijacking had occurred. These factors tend to indicate that some of the multiple hijackings were planned well in advance and that the "clustering" of hijacking may not necessarily be attributable to media coverage alone.

Diffusion Theory Possibilities

General conclusions that can be drawn from studies of diffusion of innovations in other situations do not provide much support for the view that media are crucial elements as a contagion. Mass media have been found to be best at assisting diffusion when combined with interpersonal channels and when used in reinforcing rather than persuasive roles. These findings are consistent with and an outgrowth of the two-step flow theory research of Lazarsfeld and Katz (1955) and others who have shown that interpersonal influences are much stronger than media in altering attitudes and behavior. This interpersonal-influence approach arose in the 1940s as social scientists were forced to reject the stimulus-response based theories of media effects offered in the 1930s. Those theories placed media influences on individuals very high, but were not supported by scientific research.

If one accepts general diffusion theory as having relevance to the spread of terrorism, one would have to hypothesize that media may play a role in the awareness aspect of the adoption process of terrorism, but only a minor part—at best—in the evaluative, acceptance, and adoption portions of the diffusion of terrorist techniques. Diffusion principles also provide a testable explanation for the increasing number of acts of political violence. Because they provide an established normal S-curve of cumulative adoption of innovations, researchers on terrorism could develop methods to analyze adoption of various techniques and practices to determine whether the adoption followed normal patterns or was unusual.

I do not wish to fall into the trap of using the evidence from diffusion research as conclusive evidence about the role of media in terrorism, as many terrorism researchers have done by accepting results from violence research. The general conclusions drawn from diffusion research, however, have not been the subjects of the type of heated debate that has surrounded the violence research because they have been much less contradictory and inconclusive. The diffusion principles suggest hypotheses that are well suited for testing in the realm of terrorism, although no such studies exist today that add evidence to the discussion of media and terrorism (Rogers, 1983).

It is clear, then, that no causal link has been established, using any acceptable social science research methods, between media coverage and the spread of terrorism. Without such a link, media are being unjustifiably blamed for the increasing acts of violence throughout the world.

I do not wish to be interpreted, however, as taking the position that no link can ever be established, only that one cannot do so with the state of knowledge today. The fact that media cannot be shown to be the contagion of terrorism does not exonerate them from excesses in coverage that have been shown to harm authorities' ability to cope with specific incidents of violence, have endangered the lives of victims and authorities, have been unduly sensational, and have spread fear among the public. For such errors in judgment and violations of existing industry standards, the offending media must bear the responsibility. One would hope that such problems will diminish as journalists become more acquainted with the techniques of terrorists and discuss the problems and implications of their coverage.

Coverage as a Preventative of Terrorism

If media cannot be shown to be the cause of the spread of terrorism, can they be shown to be useful in preventing or reducing the scale of violence in terrorist attacks?

One important school of thought suggests coverage may actually reduce the possibility of future violent action on the part of those who engage in terroristic violence by removing the need for individuals and groups to resort to violence in order to gain coverage. The view that some coverage may reduce terrorism is not held solely at the fringes of the terrorism research community, although it receives little support among government officials and those to whom they most often turn for advice in combating terrorism. Abraham H. Miller (1982), who has written extensively on legal issues involving media during terrorist incidents, notes the major elements of the view: "If terrorism is a means of reaching the public forum, violence can be defused by providing accessibility to the media without the necessity of an entry fee of blood and agony" (p. 24). Indeed, this was a conclusion reached at a conference on 'errorism at Ditchley Castle in Oxfordshire, England, in 1978.

Another conclusion urging full, complete, and serious media coverage of such violence was reached by the Task Force on Disorders and Terrorism, which noted that

> the media can be most influential in setting the tone for a proper response by the civil authorities to disorders, acts of terrorism, and political violence. It can provide an outlet for the expression of legitimate public concern on important issues so as to act as a safety valve, and it can bring pressure to bear in response to public sentiment in an effective manner to redress grievances and to change official policies. (National Advisory Committee, 1977, p. 65)

The response to the problem of terrorism should be more, not less, news coverage, the task force argued: "The news media should devote more, rather than less, space and attention to the phenomena of extraordinary violence" (p. 368). If such coverage avoids glamorizing the perpetrators of violence, provides reliable information, and gives appropriate emphasis to the consequences of violence, it will increase public understanding, reduce public fear, and assist in reducing violence, the report indicated.

These conclusions were reached by the task force despite the fact that it generally accepted a stimulus-response view of media effects. Although admitting that no authoritative evidence directly linked media and violence, the group accepted the premises that media directly or indirectly influence potential perpetrators of violence and potential victims and that coverage of such violence affects the ability of authorities to respond.

If one accepts the view that unrequited grievances, frustration, and despair lead to political rebellion, and that those who rebel are denied forums in media because media are institutions that support and perpetuate the dominant political order of the states in which they operate, one must conclude that normal media channels are regularly denied to these extreme dissidents.

This being the case, the only possible avenues left for gaining a media forum are acts designed to force their way into the forums. Violence, as we are all too painfully aware, is an effective way of achieving such forums.

The provision-of-forums-as-a-means-of-combating-terrorism view holds that reasonable provision of forums in noncoerced environments may help reduce the frustration that leads to such violent acts and lead to an understanding of the issues or points of view of the dissidents. Two psychologists who conduct research in the area of terrorism, Jeffrey Rubin of Tufts University and Nehemia Friedland of Tel Aviv University and the Project on Terrorism at the Jaffee Center for Strategic Studies, argued that governments should help provide access, which would be necessary in most nations where broadcasting is government operated or government related. The two argued:

> Governments should also try to reduce the destructiveness of terrorism by making it clear that a less dramatic performance will suffice to get the desired audience attention. Cameo appearances, for example, might be invited or encouraged as a substitute for full-scale productions [terrorist theater]. Imagine that Yasir Arafat or George Habash were to be invited to meet the press on Israeli television to express their views on what they consider to be political reality in the Middle East. Such an arrangement would provide these actors with the element of legitimacy they seek and would air issues without resorting to anything more violent than the savagery of the Israeli news media. (Rubin & Friedland, 1986, p. 28)

As with most of the theories surrounding the role of media in terrorism, there is little supporting evidence—only intuition—bolstering this free-expression-as-a-means-of-controlling-violence theory. The theory has merit and deserves to be studied closely, however, as do the principles from the diffusion approach.

Several possible studies come to mind here, including behavioral analyses of groups whose views have been carried by media without coercion. In recent times, members of IRA, Palestinian, Basque, Red Army Faction, and other groups have received platforms to express their views through interviews and other forums. A study of the behavior of these groups in the periods after such interviews would be enlightening. One would hypothesize that the behavior would become less spectacularly violent after the forums were provided—a hypothesis borne out by casual observation in the case of Yasser Arafat's supporters since international forums were provided for the PLO in the 1970s.

It would appear to be inappropriate for journalists to interview members of groups taking part in terrorist acts while such acts are under way. This type of interview has occurred during the course of hijackings, building sieges, kidnappings, and other prolonged acts of terrorism. Interviews under such conditions are a direct reward for the specific act of terrorism underway and can interfere with efforts to resolve the crisis. There is also some evidence that such coverage can prolong crises. In addition, such interviews all too often increase the spectacle of the event, spread fear, and provide a coerced platform for the views of the groups involved.

I do not believe, however, that interviews not conducted during a specific event need be treated in the same manner, despite protestations to the contrary by government officials. Interviews such as those of Abul Abbas and Martin McGuinness, mentioned at the beginning of this chapter, clearly do not provide a reward for a specific violent act, do not interfere with authorities' efforts to control a specific incident, do not endanger the lives of any hostages or authorities attempting to cope with hostage situations, and obviously cannot prolong a specific crisis when none exists. If the coverage-as-a-preventative-measure theory is correct, such interviews should be helpful.

When such coverage is provided, however, journalists should not allow their media to become mere propaganda vehicles for those who engage in violence. Such occasions should be used as a means of exploring the causes and factors that lead to violence, of discussing policy options, and of encouraging nonviolent alternatives. This means that the journalist must exercise control and judgment in the interview, not allowing the subject of the interview to control the topics covered or the time spent on specific issues. The journalist must steer the subject away from overtly propagandistic statements with probing, serious questions aimed at getting to the heart of the issues; that is, the journalist must truly question the interviewee, not merely provide a forum.

I am not sanguine about the idea of forums being provided to terrorists, however. The idea of opening media to alienated and disenfranchised persons and groups as a means of reducing violence seems preferable to nearly any other option for controlling violence, but the chances of the idea being widely accepted are very slim. The media themselves would be reluctant to do so out of fear of offending audiences and experiencing revenue losses, as well as fears of being accused of supporting terrorists. A measure of existence of this disapprobation can be seen in the criticism heaped on NBC by other media and journalists after the Abbas interview.

In addition, media are not likely to convey much information conflicting with the views of the government in the nation in which they operate, or that is likely to create a conflict between the media and the government. Philip Schlesinger has noted that media generally reflect their government's perspectives when covering terrorism—regardless of the type of state in which they exist—and that perspectives that conflict with the government's views are rarely carried (Schlesinger, Murdock, & Elliot, 1983).

As a result of such problems, I believe it will be difficult to convince government officials and their terrorism advisers that media may possibly aid the campaign against terrorist violence.

Summary

The lack of scientifically acceptable evidence about media and terrorism and the absence of criticism of the scanty and questionable evidence about media effects that is offered by some government officials, security advisers, and researchers leave media open to significant attacks by legislators and executive agencies.

Because there will be continuing terrorism in the years to come and no projected decline in such activity, there is great danger ahead for media in all nations that suffer from terrorist attacks. Movement toward restricting the flow of information through media is gaining momentum, backed by dubious studies couched in the scientific jargon of the social sciences. Most officials and members of the public do not know enough to be able to question this evidence.

Those of us in the social sciences who appreciate and understand the contributions of media to society have a duty to help the public and officials part the veil of ignorance that shrouds the subject of terrorism and the media. We must help set and undertake a research agenda that can be realistically expected to answer the serious charges and questions about journalism's roles in the spread of terrorism.

I do not mean that we should start with our own set of biases to "prove" that the media are innocent. But we do need to set out to find out just what the reality is. I suspect we will find that media are a contributing factor in the spread of terrorism, just as easy international transportation, the easy availability of weapons and explosives, the intransigence of some governments' policies, the provision of funds to terrorists by a variety of supportive governments, and a host of other factors are to blame. Whatever the results of our research, it will move us closer to reality than the views offered by those who argue that the media are wholly at fault and those who argue that media are blameless. The resulting knowledge will make it less likely that governments will act precipitously to control media coverage and more likely that journalists will gain a better understanding of terrorism that will leave them less open to manipulation and more aware of the consequences of their actions.

References

Bassiouni, M. C. (1983). Problems of media coverage of nonstate-sponsored terror-violence incidents. In L. Z. Freedman & Y. Alexander (Eds.), *Perspectives on terrorism* (p. 184). Wilmington, DE: Scholarly Resources.

Bellmann, J. (1986, January). BBC: Clearing the air. *The Journalist*, p. 20.

Boyer, P. J. (1986). Arab's interview stirs news debate. *New York Times*, May 7, p. A7.

Grossman, L. (1986, July). The face of terrorism. *The Quill*, p. 38.

Heyman, E., & Mickolus, E. (1980, June). Observations on "Why violence spreads." *International Studies Quarterly*, pp. 299-305.

Jenkins, B. M. (1981, June). *The psychological implications of media-covered terrorism.* (The Rand Paper Series P-6627). Santa Monica, CA: Rand Corporation.

Lazarsfeld, P., & Katz, E. (1955). *Personal influence: The part played by people in mass communications.* Glencoe, IL: Free Press.

Levy, R. (1985, October-December). Terrorism and the mass media. *Military Intelligence,* p. 35.

Midlarsky, M. I., Crenshaw, M., & Yoshida, F. (1980, June). Why violence spreads: The contagion of international terrorism. *International Studies Quarterly,* p. 276.

Miller, A. H. (1982). *Terrorism: The media and the law.* Dobbs Ferry, NY: Transnational.

National Advisory Committee on Criminal Justice Standards and Goals, Disorders and Terrorism. (1977). *Report of the Task Force on Disorders and Terrorism.* Washington, DC: Law Enforcement Assistance Administration.

Rabe, R. L. (1977). Terrorism and the media. In Y. Alexander & S. M. Finger (Eds.), *Terrorism: Interdisciplinary perspectives* (p. 69). New York: John Jay.

Rogers, E. M. (1983). *Communication of innovations: A cross-cultural approach* (3rd ed.). New York: Free Press.

Rubin, J. Z., & Friedland, N. (1986, March). Theater of terror. *Psychology Today.*

Schlesinger, P., Murdock, G., & Elliot, P. (1983). *Televising "terrorism": Political violence in popular culture.* London: Comedia.

Schmid, A. P., & de Graaf, J. (1982). *Violence as communication: Insurgent terrorism and the western news media.* Beverly Hills, CA: Sage.

Thatcher urges the press to help "starve" terrorists. (1985). *New York Times,* July 16, p. A3.

6

Network Evening News Coverage of the TWA Hostage Crisis

TONY ATWATER

A series of international terrorist activities during the 1980s has focused attention on the role of the media in publicizing such incidents. In 1985 and 1986 the television networks devoted extensive news coverage to the TWA hostage crisis, the *Achille Lauro* hijacking, the Malta debacle, and the Rome/Vienna airport bombings. By providing extensive and continuous coverage of terrorist events, television networks risk giving a platform to terrorist grievances. Laqueur (1977) has asserted that the success of a terrorist operation depends heavily on the amount of publicity it receives.

The potential for becoming participants in terrorist acts calls for additional discretion on the part of television journalists. In the political arena, media coverage of terrorist activities has sometimes been interpreted as an element of pressure on government to resolve promptly what citizens may regard as a national crisis. Alexander (1978) has observed that through excessive news coverage "establishment" communications channels willingly or unwillingly become tools in the terrorist strategy.

Adams (1982) has noted that the accusation that excessive media coverage legitimizes terrorist interests warrants documentation before

AUTHOR'S NOTE: Reprinted from *Journalism Quarterly*, Vol. 64, Nos. 2 and 3 (Summer-Autumn), 1987, with permission of the Association for Education in Journalism and Mass Communication.

we can accept such a charge as factual. The purpose of this chapter was to investigate the amount and nature of news coverage devoted to the hijacking of Transworld Airlines (TWA) Flight 847 on June 14, 1985. Studies on media coverage of hostage crises help journalists and consumers to become more knowledgeable about conventions in news coverage of international terrorism.

The daily network news broadcasts provide a major outlet upon which many Americans rely for news of the day. Further, the agenda-setting potential of television warrants that social scientists explore audience implications of detailed coverage of terrorism (Shaw & Mc-Combs, 1977). An individual network's daily news coverage of a hostage crisis may send a message to viewers by the emphasis that the evening news gives the event. This chapter analyzed the extent of coverage that the networks devoted to a terrorist event in their evening news broadcasts. The study is unique in its analysis of the complete time period of the crisis from the seizure of the American hostages aboard TWA Flight 847 (June 14, 1985) until their release (June 30, 1985). The study adds to earlier analyses of network news coverage of crises that have attempted to convey insight into the nature, rationale, and emphasis of network news content on terrorism.

Related Studies

Several previous studies have examined network evening news coverage of the Iranian hostage crisis of 1979. Altheide (1982) found no significant differences among the networks in the number of reports and topics covered relative to the crisis. He noted that reports on the instability and volatility of the Iranian government character-ized the evening news broadcasts of all three networks. In another study of the Iranian hostage crisis, Meeske and Javaheri (1982) again found similarity among the networks in that they were neutral in terms of expressing bias for or against the United States and Iran.

In a later study Altheide (1985) found that certain topics received varied amounts of network coverage during the Iranian hostage crisis. He observed that the reporting of selected events corresponded with criteria of production formats such as visual quality, thematic unity, and accessibility. Similarity in organization and format among networks contributed to consonance or homogeneity in network reports of the hostage crisis.

Although much has been written about the similarity of how the networks covered the Iranian hostage crisis, Nimmo and Combs (1985, p. 165) reported that the three networks exhibited differing thematic emphases and foci of coverage. The authors also noted that the networks differed in the persons selected as news sources. NBC, for example, was found to have relied more heavily on average citizens in the network's reports on the crisis.

Paletz, Ayanian, and Fozzard (1982, pp. 143-165) studied network coverage of three terrorist groups and found that the networks reported the same events and portrayed them similarly. The researchers concluded that television news did not endow terrorists with legitimacy and that the justness of terrorist causes was denied. A fault of network coverage, according to the authors, was its failure to reflect adequately upon the underlying objectives behind terrorist acts.

Research Questions

The period examined was June 14-30, 1985, which encompassed the day on which the hostages were seized through the time of their eventual release. The extent of coverage devoted to reports on the hostage crisis was the central issue to be investigated. Several specific research questions that the study addressed included the following:

(1) What was the amount of coverage devoted to the crisis daily in each network's evening news broadcast?

(2) What types of stories did hostage reports frequently involve (anchor, reporter, commentary)?

(3) What topics did the evening news broadcasts emphasize in covering the TWA hostage crisis?

(4) What percentage of news time did network evening newscasts devote to the crisis daily?

(5) Where did most reports on the TWA hostage crisis originate?

Method

A comprehensive content analysis of TWA hostage reports broadcast on *ABC World News Tonight, CBS Evening News,* and *NBC Nightly News* was undertaken to address the above issues. Comprehensive, compiled videotapes of these reports were obtained from the Vanderbilt University Television News Archive. All TWA hostage stories broadcast by the evening news programs between June 14, 1985, and June 30, 1985, were included in the analysis. Each story was coded with the aid of a two-page protocol for story type, story topic, origin of report, length of story, and network identification. The unit of analysis was the news story, which was defined as "any topic introduced by the anchor person coupled with any report or reports by other correspondents on the same topic and any concluding remarks by the anchor person" (Fowler & Showalter, 1974). Each news item was coded according to type as either an anchor story, reporter story, or commentary/analysis. This typology was used to specify the main presenter of the story and to distinguish news items from commentaries (Nimmo & Combs, 1985, p. 165).

Story Topic

Each TWA hostage story was coded into one of 17 topic categories according to the topic that was principally featured in the report. Several of the topic categories were developed after a preliminary review of videotapes and news transcripts. The other topic categories used in the analysis were based on Altheide's (1982) study of the Iranian hostage crisis.

Story Origin

To ascertain the proximity with which stories were filed on the crisis, four categories were used to describe story origin. Those categories included: (a) Washington/New York; (b) USA/Other; (c) Beirut/Lebanon; and (d) London/Other. Because all three network newscasts typically originate from New York, anchor-read stories were coded Washington/New York unless reported from another location. An additional category, Location Not Given, was used when a report other than an anchor-read story failed to indicate place of origin. The category USA/Other was assigned to stories from U.S. cities other than Washington, D.C., or New York. The category London/Other was assigned to those stories filed from London and other cities and countries other than London, England, and Beirut, Lebanon.

Table 6.1 Number of Network Hostage Reports by Day

Newscast Day	ABC	CBS	NBC	Total
June 14	6	6	9	21
June 15	11	13	6	30
June 16	14	13	13	40
June 17	13	11	10	34
June 18	17	10	12	39
June 19	12	9	8	29
June 20	12	9	11	32
June 21	6	8	7	21
June 22	6	5	5	16
June 23	12	7	8	27
June 24	9	6	9	24
June 25	15	7	9	31
June 26	12	9	11	32
June 27	8	11	9	28
June 28	7	7	7	21
June 29	13	13	11	37
June 30	8	13	8	29
Total	181	157	153	491

$\chi^2 = 13.39$, df = 32, N.S.

News Time

Each hostage story broadcast on the three evening newscasts was coded in seconds with the aid of a stopwatch. In addition, a measure of the "news hole" for each of the 51 newscasts was computed by eliminating time devoted to commercials. This computation was assisted by the use of network newscast transcripts and the Television News Index and Abstracts (Vanderbilt Television News Archives, 1985). The percentage of news time devoted to TWA stories by day was computed as a ratio of TWA story time and news hole time.

Intercoder reliability estimates were obtained for story type and story topic. Two judges independently coded a random sample of 20 TWA hostage stories. The reliability estimates obtained from this procedure were 90% for story type and 90% for story topic.

Table 6.2 Network Hostage Reports by Story Type (Percentage)

Story Type	ABC	CBS	NBC
Anchor	90 (49.7)	75 (47.8)	76 (49.7)
Reporter	73 (40.3)	8 (43.3)	63 (41.2)
Commentary/Analysis	18 (9.9)	14 (8.9)	14 (9.2)
Total (N = 491)	181	157	153

Table 6.3 Origin of Network Hostage Reports by Percentage

Origin	ABC	CBS	NBC
Washington/New York	65.7	63.1	67.3
USA/Other	5.0	5.1	5.2
Beirut/Lebanon	12.7	10.2	16.3
London/Other	16.0	17.8	11.1
Location Not Given	0.6	3.8	0.0
Total	181	157	153

Results

The network evening news broadcasts devoted extensive coverage to the TWA hostage crisis. A total of 491 hostage stories were broadcast over the 17-day crisis period, comprising approximately 12 hours of news time. Table 6.1 lists the total number of hostage reports broadcast on each evening news program during each day of the crisis. ABC's evening newscast reported the largest number of hostage stories, 181, compared to 157 stories by CBS and 153 by NBC. The data show that the amount of coverage given the crisis among the networks was similar from one day to the next ($p - .001$). These findings are consistent with those reported in earlier analyses of network coverage of the Iranian hostage crisis.

In terms of story type, TWA hostage stories were most frequently anchor stories. However, Table 6.2 indicates that hostage stories presented by the reporter were also frequent. Approximately half of the news items presented by all three networks were anchor stories, whereas only 9% of the items involved commentary or analysis.

Table 6.4 Network Hostage Reports by Story Topic

Topic	ABC	CBS	NBC	Total
Hostage Status	58	62	48	168
U.S. Government Reaction	30	23	30	83
Israel Diplomacy	18	15	11	44
Terrorist Demands/Acts	14	9	14	37
Hostage Families	15	6	13	34
Retaliation Options	14	9	10	33
Nabih Berri/Mediation	8	10	4	22
Airport Security	3	6	8	17
Syria Mediation	6	3	4	13
Citizen Reaction/Media	7	6	1	14
Kidnapped Seven	0	5	2	7
Lebanon: Internal Problems	1	0	4	5
U.S./Israel Diplomacy	2	1		4
Private Diplomacy	0	0	1	1
Islam/Culture	2		0	4
Lebanon: External Problems	2	0	2	4
World Reaction	1	0		1
Total	181	157	153	491

$\chi^2 = 38.54$, df = 32, NS

Again the evidence suggests consonance in the nature of the news content devoted to the hostage crisis.

The overwhelming majority of hostage stories were filed from Washington and New York. Over 65% of the stories originated from these two national network headquarters. Table 6.3 shows that Beirut was the third most frequent place of origin for reports on the crisis. Almost 13% of hostage stories originated from the Lebanese capital.

Topical Emphasis

Among the 17 topics used in the analysis, Hostage Status and U.S. Government Reaction were the most frequently involved in stories on the TWA hijacking. Table 6.4 lists the number of reports involving each topic. The category Hostage Status accounted for 34% of all hostage stories, whereas U.S. Government Reaction accounted for almost 17%. The topics Hostage Families, Israel Diplomacy, and Terrorist Demands/Acts also received emphasis in the network evening

Table 6.5 Minutes of Network Hostage Reports by Day (Percentage)

Newscast Day	ABC		CBS		NBC	
June 14	10.7	(50.3)	10.0	(46.7)	12.5	(58.6)
June 15	14.6	(70.0)	14.7	(68.3)	14.5	(55.3)
June 16	17.6	(94.9)	19.0	(89.8)	15.8	(73.4)
June 17	19.1	(89.5)	19.2	(88.6)	15.8	(75.4)
June 18	19.9	(91.0)	14.7	(67.5)	16.6	(76.7)
June 19	20.6	(95.8)	7.6	(35.2)	13.0	(61.4)
June 20	17.0	(77.9)	17.5	(84.2)	18.1	(86.6)
June 21	14.3	(66.0)	11.2	(51.5)	10.6	(49.0)
June 22	10.2	(48.7)	6.9	(32.2)	6.0	(42.6)
June 23	9.5	(46.9)	11.6	(53.6)	15.2	(70.7)
June 24	13.9	(64.6)	9.3	(43.0)	12.1	(55.9)
June 25	14.9	(67.6)	8.2	(37.6)	13.2	(63.7)
June 26	19.2	(90.0)	13.6	(62.1)	13.7	(65.4)
June 27	15.0	(68.6)	14.4	(65.6)	14.1	(65.9)
June 28	13.5	(63.8)	14.3	(54.0)	11.6	(54.0)
June 29	17.6	(84.2)	19.2	(87.9)	16.3	(76.6)
June 30	12.8	(95.2)	22.3	(97.8)	15.9	(79.6)
Total	260.4		233.7		235.0	

(Total Hostage Story Time: 729.1 Minutes)

news reports. The evidence again suggested homogeneity in the topical emphasis of network evening news programs.

News Time Devoted to the Hostage Crisis

An average of 14 minutes per newscast was devoted to hostage crisis stories over the 17-day period. In addition, an average of about 9.6 news items on the crisis were featured in each of the 51 newscasts. Table 6.5 lists the news time (in minutes) given hostage reports for each day of the crisis. In parentheses on the right is the percentage of newscast time (news hole time) consumed by hostage stories on each of the 17 days examined. These data indicate once more that hostage coverage comprised large proportions of newscast time throughout the crisis period. The data also show that the proportions of the news hole consumed by hostage reports were similar among the evening news programs.

Discussion

A comprehensive visual analysis of network evening news reports broadcast during the TWA hostage crisis indicates that crisis coverage was extensive and continuous. The findings suggest that the hostage crisis was the dominant news event covered over the study period. Most hostage stories were anchor reports originating from Washington or New York. Topics that were most often involved in hostage stories were those topics about the plight of the hostages and U.S. government reaction to the crisis. Little attention was focused on less dramatic topics such as the history of Lebanon and conditions that may have given rise to the TWA hijacking. These findings strongly indicate that TWA crisis coverage on network evening newscasts was dramatic, reactive, and extensive. This trend in crisis reporting is similar to that portrayed in network evening news accounts of the Iranian hostage crisis. Limited reporting on factors that may have given rise to the crisis suggests that the broadcasts could have played a greater role as interpreters and educators in this instance.

The large proportion of news time devoted to the crisis on the three news broadcasts raises the issue of balance in reporting news of the day. The dominant play that the hostage crisis received might have influenced the issue priorities of newscast viewers. Future research should explore the extent (if any) to which newscast crisis coverage influences the issue agendas of viewers and their perceptions of reality.

References

Adams, W. C. (1982). *Television coverage of international affairs*. Norwood, NJ: Ablex.

Alexander, Y. (1978, Spring/Summer). Terrorism, the media and the police. *Journal of International Affairs, 32*, 101-113.

Altheide, D. L. (1985, Summer). Impact of format and ideology on TV news coverage of Iran. *Journalism Quarterly, 62*, 346-351.

Altheide, D. L. (1982, Autumn). Three-in-one news: Network coverage of Iran. *Journalism Quarterly, 59*, 482-486.

Fowler, J. S., & Showalter, S. W. (1974, Winter). Evening network news selection: A confirmation of news judgment. *Journalism Quarterly, 51*, 712-715.

Laqueur, W. (1977). *Terrorism: A study of national and international political violence*. Boston: Little, Brown.

Meeske, M. D., & Javaheri, M. H. (1982, Winter). Network television coverage of the Iranian hostage crisis. *Journalism Quarterly, 59*, 641-645.

Nimmo, D., & Combs, J. E. (1985). *Nightly horrors: Crisis coverage by television network news*. Knoxville: University of Tennessee Press.

Paletz, D. L., Ayanian, J. Z., & Fozzard, P. A. (1982). Terrorism on TV news: The IRA, the FALN, and the Red Brigades. In W. C. Adams (Ed.), *Television coverage of international affairs*. Norwood, NJ: Ablex.

Shaw, D. L., & McCombs, M. E. (1977). *Emergence of American political issues: The agenda-setting function of the press*. St. Paul, MN: West.

Vanderbilt Television News Archive. (1985). *Television news index and abstracts: A guide to the videotape collection of the network evening news programs in the Vanderbilt Television News Archive*. Nashville, TN: Joint University Libraries.

7

Terrorism at the BBC

The IRA on British Television

JOHN DAVID VIERA

Contemporary terrorists have put the broadcast media in a difficult position over how to cover terrorism without advancing terrorism's goals. On May 5, 1986, *NBC Nightly News* interviewed Abul Abbas, secretary general of the Palestine Liberation Front. Abbas was under indictment in the United States for the October 1985 hijacking of the Italian cruise ship Achille Lauro, which resulted in the murder of an American passenger, Leon Klinghoffer. In his two-minute interview, Abbas described President Reagan as enemy "number one" and vowed to import terrorism to the United States by attacking Americans in their own country. U.S. State Department officials quickly denounced NBC and stressed that because liberal governments agree that a new mode of terrorism has emerged that depends on media exposure, there may be times when the public good is best served through deliberate "non-exposure" by the press (Dowling, 1986, p. 14; Laqueur, 1979, p. 57; Weimann, 1987, p. 21).

This argument for non-exposure has long been espoused by the British government. In this chapter, I propose to consider the relationship of terrorism and television in the context of the British government's responses to media coverage of Irish Republican Army

AUTHOR'S NOTE: Copyright of this chapter is held by John David Viera.

(IRA) terrorist activity. One such episode centered on the British Broadcasting Corporation (BBC) and its proposed broadcast of a documentary, "At the Edge of the Union," which included an interview with Martin McGuinness, an IRA leader. The film was banned by the BBC's board of governors after political pressure from the Thatcher government during the summer of 1985. The ban led to a nationwide strike by the BBC and ITV employees and culminated with the revelation that the British security service, MI5, had been secretly approving the hiring and firing of BBC staff for years (Leigh & Lashmar, 1985a, p. 1).

Besides the issue of the government's censorship of the BBC and its implications for a free press, there is the dilemma of how the media can conduct interviews with terrorists so as not to further the cause of terrorism itself. This study will argue that cinema verité documentary techniques may very well fuel the terrorist cause and position the media in opposition to the best interests of society. There are solutions to this problem, however, using techniques of press mediation that do not involve government censorship and that avoid politicizing the media in undemocratic ways. Even so, the media are placed in a difficult political and moral position, given that both terrorists and media desire attention from a mass audience. Also, contemporary terrorist activity is purposely structured to meet the needs of television news by, for example, fulfilling conditions such as violence, intensity, unambiguity, and rarity, which according to Galtung and Ruge (1973, pp. 62-73) closely fit notions of newsworthiness as defined by news agencies (Hartley, 1982, pp. 76-79).

Background—Britain and the IRA

At the end of the 1960s, the phenomenon of international terrorism surfaced as a number of groups that used violence for political reasons began to gain media attention: the Red Army Faction (the Baader—Meinhof gang) in West Germany, the United Red Army in Japan, the Red Brigades in Italy, the Palestine Liberation Organization (PLO) in numerous places, and the IRA in Britain (Schlesinger, Murdock, & Elliot, 1983, p. 3).

In 1972, an explosion near a British Army officers' mess in Aldershot marked the arrival of the Irish Republican Army's terrorist campaign in England itself. Seven people were killed. In 1973, British authorities recorded 86 terrorist incidents, resulting in one death and 380 injuries. In 1974, casualties escalated to 45 deaths caused by political violence, including 21 people who died as the result of the bombing of two crowded pubs in Birmingham (Jaehnig, 1982, pp. 108-109).

The Birmingham bombings resulted in the passage of antiterrorist legislation—the Prevention of Terrorism (Temporary Provisions) Act 1974—that banned public displays of support for the IRA and increased the powers of the police in areas such as arrest, detention, and security checks of travelers. Although the act was not aimed at the media, some of its provisions could be interpreted as applying to journalists. In fact, during the late 1970s, the government threatened on several occasions to use the Prevention of Terrorism Act against the media for its coverage of terrorism in Northern Ireland (Jaehnig, 1982, p. 109).

British television conducted very few interviews with members of the IRA during the 1970s and 1980s (Curtis, 1986, p. 47). Each time an interview took place, there was a political row at Westminster. The summer of 1985 was no exception. A major controversy developed when "At the Edge of the Union," a 45-minute documentary on Northern Ireland, was scheduled to be shown on BBC's *Real Lives* series.

The Sequence of Events

In March 1985, Paul Hamann produced a film that investigated the 16 years of violence in the city of Derry (known as Londonderry to the Protestants) by contrasting and comparing the lives and beliefs of two of the rival leaders: Martin McGuinness, known to be the chief of staff of the outlawed IRA and a member of the Sinn Fein Irish Nationalist party, and Gregory Campbell, a militant Loyalist who believed in a Northern Ireland linked to Britain. Both men were members of the Northern Ireland Assembly.

At the time, the televising of terrorism was already controversial. In June 1985, armed Shiites had hijacked a TWA jet and the American networks had been criticized for giving too much publicity to the hijackers (TV and the hostage crisis, p. 7; TV examines its excess, p. 61). In July, British Prime Minister Margaret Thatcher had taken up the theme in a speech delivered to an American Bar Association conference in London: "We must try to find ways to starve the terrorists of the oxygen of publicity on which they depend" (Leigh & Lashmar, 1985a, p. 1).

On July 27, the Thatcher government reacted to the planned screening of "At the Edge of the Union" by demanding an explanation from the BBC concerning the film (Week in focus, 1985, p. 17). On July 28, the Sunday papers carried Thatcher's reaction to the scheduled broadcast: "Thatcher Slams IRA Film" (Penrose & Hosenball, 1985, p. 1), and "Thatcher Anger at BBC" (Week in focus, p. 17).

On Monday morning, July 29, Leon Britain, the home secretary, wrote a personal letter to the chairman of the BBC's board of governors, Stuart Young, in which he asked that the program not be shown. Even though he had not seen the film, Britain claimed that "the BBC would be giving an immensely valuable platform to those who evinced an ability to murder indiscriminately" (Betrayal on the third floor, 1985, p. 9).

On Tuesday morning, July 30, Stuart Young convened an emergency meeting of the board of governors. The governors heard the BBC's board of management's case for showing the film, which the head of the BBC documentary unit had described as "careful, thoughtful and informative," and as a balanced piece of work ("BBC delays showing banned film," 1985, p. 1). After screening the film, the governors stated it would be "unwise" to show it and publicly banned the film. The press angrily charged that the governors, many of whom were appointed during Thatcher's term, were allowing the government to dictate BBC policy (Leigh & Lashmar, 1985a, p. 1; 1985b, p. 9).

On Thursday, August 1, the governors' chairman, Stuart Young, tried to soothe the conflict between the governors and the board of management, who were pressuring the governors to reverse their decision to ban the film. BBC management took the position that "the independence of the BBC is more important than any single programme" (Week in focus, p. 17).

On Monday, August 5, broadcast journalists in Britain and Northern Ireland met to consider a possible strike. The BBC's senior management met to discuss the option of mass resignation, and the crisis escalated. BBC journalists voted to strike on Wednesday, August 7, the day the film was originally scheduled to be broadcast, unless the ban was lifted. Journalists at Independent Television News (ITN), Channel 4 News, and the National Union of Journalists voted to join the one-day strike (Marks, 1985, p. 5).

The board of governors met Tuesday, August 6, but remained adamant about the ban. On August 7, more than 2,000 BBC journalists and technicians staged a 24-hour strike. The strike stopped most television and radio newscasts in Britain (Marks, 1985, p. 5). This furor ended with the governors agreeing to run the film later in the year with some alterations and changes ("BBC delays showing banned film," 1985, p. 1).

Then followed a most extraordinary revelation. On August 18, the *Observer* broke an exclusive story charging that the British intelligence service, MI5, had secretly controlled the hiring and firing of BBC staff for years (Leigh & Lashmar, 1985a, p. 1; 1985b, p. 9). The *Observer* published case histories of eight persons who had been blacklisted by MI5 (Leigh & Lashmar, 1985a, p. 1). A new conflict, as bitter as that surrounding the McGuinness film and perhaps even more ominous, enveloped the BBC.

The National Union of Journalists warned BBC management of a "head-on conflict" if evaluation and approval of its members by MI5 did not cease (Rayment, 1985, p. .3). This new scandal pushed the banned film out of the media limelight. Almost two months later, on October 16, 1985, the controversy over "At the Edge of the Union" ended when the film was broadcast unchanged, except for the addition of 19 seconds of archival footage of victims of an IRA bombing in Belfast.

Media, Access, and Terrorism

Broadcast journalism's coverage of terrorism is caught in the middle of a very complex situation, where even the choice of words becomes crucial. Terrorist rhetoric stresses political motivations and the adoption of a self-conscious media strategy, referring to its members as "freedom fighters," "guerrillas," or "members of the resistance." For the IRA, there is a state of war. For the government, a war confers legitimacy on the enemy; thus, there is no war, the violence is criminal and violates the law (Schlesinger et al., 1983, p. 4). In this battle of rhetoric, broadcast journalists can retain a middle ground if they choose their words carefully, but they must remember that terrorism and its portrayal are always in danger of becoming theater, of turning news into dramatic entertainment (Schmid & de Graaf, 1982, p. 69; Sperry, 1976, p. 141).

The dilemma facing media coverage of terrorism centers on the issue of media access. Governments claim media exposure fuels terrorism, except perhaps for showing its victims and its bloody aftermath. Denial of access—the nonexposure position—potentially disenfranchises terrorists, makes "them" invisible. Making media access easier, on balance, would be unwelcome to governments, as such coverage would tend to authenticate and legitimate both the terrorists and their cause. But invisibility demands violent acts of terrorism in order for their cause to be noticed. Proponents of public-forum theory argue that lack of media exposure fuels terrorism (Bell, 1978, p. 50).

For example, one commentator argues that media coverage could be construed as a nonviolent alternative, a release for terrorist energy (Miller, 1982, pp. 24-27). It is argued that bloodshed results from the need for terrorists to gain notoriety; thus making the media accessible will perhaps cut down on violent acts by terrorists. From a governmental point of view, there are pros and cons to this suggestion. The elimination of bloodshed would be welcome, but what is really desired is the elimination of the terrorists themselves, along with their cause (which is almost always anti-government or caused by governmental actions). On the other hand, media coverage of violent acts helps to relate terrorism to criminality. This is why governments encourage aftermath footage (as added to "At the Edge of the Union") but decry nonviolent portrayals that tend to humanize (e.g., images in the film of McGuinness with his child).

There are functional benefits to access. For one thing, terrorists and governments have an open channel for communication, a means for an indirect dialogue. For another, media coverage can solidify the public against the terrorists' violent acts, which, though politically motivated are nevertheless criminal as well (Week in focus, 1985, p. 17). This assumes there is no humanistic coverage, including nonantagonistic interviews that can imply legitimacy.

The options for liberal societies seem to be either government restrictions on the media as a necessary part of the government's campaign against terrorism or voluntary restraint or self-regulation by the news media. We do know that most democratic states so far have resisted the step of overt censorship. Authorities on terrorism, according to Dowling (1986, p. 22), view "prior restraints on the media and enactment of repressive law enforcement measures as unacceptable prices to pay for solution of the threat posed by terrorism." However, it remains "advantageous for the state to adopt an information policy which integrates the media into a national-security design," thus encouraging an indirect censorship (Schlesinger et al., 1983, p. 143). Such incorporation preserves the public illusion of an independent media system while insuring that the media picks "us" over "them." Both overt censorship and this type of indirect censorship present dangers for a free-press democracy. As one British writer has stated: "One of the reasons why terrorism is such a virulent poison is that the cure can damage society as much as the disease can" (Jaehnig, 1982, p. 106).

Censorship

The relationship between media and government is often phrased antagonistically. In Western democracies, the media are supposed to be public watchdogs, applying their investigative powers to restrain and critique government activity rather than functioning as propaganda machines on the government's behalf. In fact, however, the relationship between government and press tends to be far cozier than the myth would allow (Miller, 1982, pp. 13-49).

For one thing, the broadcast media are regulated by the government. For another, both press and broadcast media are dependent on government sources for information, particularly in crisis situations (e.g., in the Falklands or Grenada). And further, the government often sets the agenda for the media. In the case of the BBC, this relationship is even more intimate because the BBC, through an independent governmental agency, is also the nation's flagship station, Britain's national network. Thus the agenda for BBC news and documentary programming is closely related to government concerns. In the case of Northern Ireland, it is an open question how free and independent the BBC will be allowed to be (Jaehnig, 1982, pp. 106-122). From the American point of view, the BBC exists somewhere between NBC and USIA's *Voice of America* (although not restricted to foreign audiences).

Censorship concerns arise because many media commentators do not believe that the British political structure is under real danger from IRA bombings and thus are puzzled by governmental acts to muzzle the media. Many media critics argue that if this is actual war, then censorship may be imposed and "that's fair enough because we'll all know where we stand" (Schlesinger et al., 1983, p. 65). An example is the Thatcher government's threats and attempts to use sections of the Prevention of Terrorism Act against the media (see Jaehnig, 1982, pp. 106-122).

From 1974 to 1979, no interviews with members of the provisional IRA were broadcast in Britain, over either the BBC or ITV. Two interviews were conducted with members of the Irish National Liberation Army (INLA)—one in 1977, the other in 1979 (Schlesinger et al., 1983, p. 125). The 1979 interview came in July after a March killing of an MP from Northern Ireland at the House of Commons in London. The anonymous INLA member wore a disguise and was interviewed in Dublin. A chorus of protest arose over the interview, and Thatcher ordered the attorney general to investigate the possibility of an action against the BBC under the Prevention of Terrorism Act.

Later in 1979, another incident occurred. BBC crews filmed an illegal IRA roadblock in Carrickmore in Northern Ireland. Again, there was controversy in Parliament, and Thatcher demanded that the BBC "put its house in order" (Schlesinger et al., 1983, p. 127). Setting an ominous precedent, police seized a copy of the film under the Prevention of Terrorism Act. In August 1980, the BBC was notified by the government that both the July interview and the filming of the IRA roadblock were offenses under Section 11 of the act. The film of the Carrickmore roadblock was never shown.

Outright censorship is not the British way of doing things, though such is advocated regularly by the right wing as part of the "war" against terrorism. The government never actually prosecuted the BBC for its alleged violations of Section 11, presumably because threats were enough to effectively silence the organization, which repeatedly tightened its internal controls—its self-censorship—over terrorist coverage. From the time of these incidents up until the showing of "At the Edge of the Union," the IRA and INLA were more or less invisible on the BBC, except as portrayed in "terrorist aftermath" footage (Curtis, 1986, p. 47).

A look at the BBC's internal controls concerning coverage of terrorists reveals the BBC's lack of autonomy. In 1971, both BBC and

ITV were forced to declare their loyalty to the government and eliminate the goal of impartiality. The government minister in charge of broadcasting told Parliament that equal coverage was no longer to be given to the other side. Both the BBC chairman and the head of ITV assured the Home Office that their organizations would uphold "the values and objectives of the society that they [were] there to serve" (Schlesinger et al., 1983, p. 122).

At the BBC, this commitment to government has been ensured through a "reference upwards" policy, whereby producers, reporters, and editors have to obtain permission from higher-ups as regards programs concerning Northern Ireland. This applies not only to news, current affairs, and documentaries, but also to dramatizations. Depending on the level of controversy, permission from the director general may be necessary. All interviews with terrorists must go to the director general. These internal controls have resulted in an almost total absence of interviews (eight in 12 years—four on BBC and four on ITV). The ITV network has been even more conservative than the BBC. Its actions during the 1970s included the outright banning of programs dealing with terrorism (Schlesinger et al., 1983, pp. 111-115).

These internal controls reveal a BBC and ITV so constrained regarding Northern Ireland that even a historical documentary is difficult to produce. It amounts to a de facto censorship of coverage of Northern Ireland and has threatened the notion that the BBC should provide a democratic forum as an independent entity functioning under public service principles (see Curtis, 1986, pp. 48-49).

Media and the Terrorist

Given that one function of the BBC is to supply information, and given that the government's nonexposure position amounts to the desire to have no terrorists on television except as part of clearly anti-terrorist footage, then two results are to be expected: (a) coverage of the IRA and Northern Ireland is bound to be biased toward the violent aftermath of terrorist activities (see Schlesinger et al., 1983); and (b) journalists risk being categorized as participants in the terrorist cause (or at least furthering it), rather than as objective reporters of it, for any coverage not explicitly anti-terrorist or failing to reveal the horrors of terrorist acts (see Miller, 1982).

The problem is that broadcast journalists not desiring to remain mere conduits for governmental information often become dependent on terrorists for information about terrorism. Journalists are thus trapped, unable to present objective coverage because there is no possible objectivity given the two available sources of information.

This dilemma emphasizes the debate over whether media in such circumstances should be pro-state, actively portraying the evils of terrorism, or serve as a public forum for the social debate implied by terrorism's political motives. Under the public-forum theory, the BBC is to be free from governmental control and mandated to provide information so that citizens may make informed political judgments. The BBC should be able to challenge the prevailing status quo, to articulate the unpopular, and to present the minority point of view, including programming targeted for minority audience interests. In principle, the BBC would be free to report Northern Ireland as it sees fit.

Schlesinger, Murdock, and Elliot (1983) investigated how terrorism was portrayed in the United Kingdom by "actuality" television—news, current affairs, and documentary programming. The report found that the main source of information about terrorists, news programming, operated "predominantly within the terms of the official perspective" (p. 36). Reporters tended to conduct terrorist interviews in an aggressive style, which appeared as pro-government. When there was a rare exception (such as the 1979 INLA interview described above), it "invariably provoke[d] heated debate on the legitimacy of giving airtime to enemies of the state" (Schlesinger et al., 1983, p. 40). The public-forum position remains far from a reality in Britain.

"At the Edge of the Union" is a variation of the cinema verité style of documentary, falling within the context of the "public forum" position. Cinema verité was premised on the "scientific" need for the filmmaker(s) to be invisible—that is, to allow for the presentation of unmediated reality. Although we know this is theoretically impossible (even the hidden camera has been positioned by a human consciousness), cinema verité attempts to capture objective reality as conceived by traditional physics and assumed by empiricism. This visual anthropological tool, this film technique, was adapted by American filmmakers under the banner of "direct cinema."

The cinema verité stylistic codes, which developed out of practical and technical necessities and not necessarily artistic choice, have become so associated with actuality or "truth" that they have become a kind of verification that the footage being seen is "real" (i.e., not mediated). The 1:33 to 1 aspect ratio of 16mm film, the hand-held camera, the use of available light or nonaesthetically lit images (TV news lighting style or illumination, not "lighting"), blurred or racked focus, a haphazard composition of shots—all the visual codings associated with cinema verité have become indications of the authenticity of the film footage.

The use of light-weight, hand-held cameras, which precipitated the development of the verité style in the later 1950s, coincided with the needs of TV news, which was also interested in the "truth" of surface phenomena and the immediacy of spontaneous, on-location action. The verité style was compatible with media standards of honesty, neutrality, and objectivity, and with the added desire of television for intimacy.

However, "truth" or "reality," particularly news reality, is constructed. Objectivity is not a possibility. We have acknowledged the verité style's behind-the-scenes manipulation of subject and image, particularly in editing. Nevertheless, the lack of an overt mediation continues to render the illusion that the "thing" being watched is, at the very least, authentic—apparently because we, the viewers, appear to access it directly.

Bill Nichols (1985, p. 260) identifies four major styles of documentary filmmaking: (a) the off-screen narration of the Grierson tradition; (b) the cinema verité of the 1960s; (c) the interview-oriented film of the 1970s; and (d) the new self-reflexive documentaries, where the filmmaker is a "participant-witness" and "a promoter of cinematic discourse rather than a neutral or all-knowing reporter of the way things truly are." Each style has sought to address limitations in the tradition preceding it (p. 270).

"At the Edge of the Union" incorporates both the verité and the interview-oriented mode. Nichols (1985, p. 265) argues that the interview-oriented mode was a response to the limitations of verité, to the recognition that events cannot speak for themselves. However, the interview style itself contains inherent limitations. First, the word of the interviewee tends to be uncritically accepted. The witnesses are not, according to Nichols (1985), "compelled to vouch for their own validity" (p. 265). In addition, historical understanding may be limited to the personal (p. 267). The main problem identified by Nichols is that most interview-based films do not retain "that sense of a gap between

the voice of interviewees and the voice of the text as a whole"
(p. 266).

It is this lack of a "voice of the text as a whole" and the lack of
overt mediation in the verité and interview styles that is at the root of
the controversy over "At the Edge of the Union." The government ob-
jects to the authentication of an IRA reality (i.e., to showing any footage at all) and demands a mediation technique that strips the raw
image of its power. The problem (and question) is: Is it possible in
television journalism to present the truth while simultaneously and
overtly mediating it—standing between the event and the viewer's
direct experience of it? Skilled documentarians such as Emile de An-
tonio or ethnographers David and Judith MacDougall have created
work that demonstrates, according to Nichols (1985, p. 271), this
structural sophistication, this gap between the voice of the interviewee and the voice of the text. Nichols says that by acting self-
reflexively, the strategies of these documentaries "call the status of
the interview itself into question and diminish its tacit claim to tell
the whole truth" (p. 271). However, this type of self-referential work
would most likely be considered too unconventional by TV journalists, especially when offered as TV news, which is so thoroughly
rooted in the verité and interview modes.

Documentaries in the Grierson tradition, where narration
dominates the visuals and mediation is overtly present, may be television journalists' only recourse. If they wish to avoid government
interference, British journalists can try to mediate terrorist footage as
much as possible. For example, interviewers may be overtly hostile
and unsympathetic to the terrorists and their cause. Victims of terrorist activity may be shown. A "voice of God" narration can point out
contradictions or inaccuracies in statements made by terrorists. The
government would probably be happy with any of these strategies.

But what about nonverbal meanings: the terrorist as human, with a
baby on his lap? Is it possible to report this basic truth about reality
(that terrorists are human) and thus attempt a full portrayal of the
event? The British government might be satisfied if journalists inter-
cut such footage with a denouncing live commentator or voice-over.
This is the best that can be hoped for in the situation where the media
cannot be "impartial," where it has to renounce, in effect, its own
journalistic codes of neutrality, impartiality, objectivity, balance, or
"just the facts" in the name of a "higher" good. In the case of Britain
and the IRA, it may be that a full treatment of the problem can only

be gotten from Italian, Swedish, or American television—that is, from outside the state's political boundaries. Such international impartiality may be the best we can do.

References

BBC delays showing banned film. (1985). *The Guardian*, August 9, p. 1.

Bell, J. B. (1978, May-June). Terrorist scripts and live-action spectaculars. *Columbia Journalism Review*, pp. 47-50.

Betrayal on the third floor. (1985). *The Observer*, August 4, p. 9.

Curtis, L. (1986, March-April). British broadcasting in Ireland. *Screen, 27*(2), 47-51.

Dowling, R. E. (1986, Winter). Terrorism in the media: A rhetorical genre. *Journal of Communication, 36*(1), 12-24.

Galtung, J., & Ruge, M. (1973). Structuring and selecting news. In S. Cohen & J. Young (Eds.), *The manufacture of news* (pp. 62-73). London: Constable.

Hartley, J. (1982). *Understanding news*. London: Methuen.

Jaehnig, W. (1982). Terrorism in Britain: On the limits of free expression. In A. H. Miller (Ed.), *Terrorism: The media and the law* (pp. 106-122). Dobbs Ferry, NY: Transnational.

Laqueur, W. (1979). *Terrorism*. Boston: Little.

Leigh, D., & Lashmar, P. (1985a). Revealed: How MI5 vets BBC staff. *The Observer*, August 18, p. 1.

Leigh, D., & Lashmar, P. (1985b). The blacklist in Room 105. *The Observer*, August 18, p. 9.

Marks, L. (1985). BBC turmoil over Ulster reporting. *The Observer*, August 11, p. 5.

Miller, A. H. (1982). Terrorism, the media, and the law: A discussion of the issues. In A. H. Miller (Ed.), *Terrorism: The media and the law* (pp. 13-49). Dobbs Ferry, NY: Transnational.

Nichols, B. (1985). The voice of documentary. In B. Nichols (Ed.), *Movies and methods II*. Berkeley: University of California Press.

Penrose, B., & Hosenball, M. (1985). Thatcher slams IRA film. *The Sunday Times*, August 28, p. 3.

Rayment, T. (1985). Ultimatum to BBC over MI vetting. *The Sunday Times*, August 25, p. 3.

Schlesinger, P., Murdock, G., & Elliot, P. (1983). *Televising terrorism: Political violence in popular culture*. London: Comedia.

Schmid, A. P., & de Graaf, J. (1982). *Violence as communication: Insurgent terrorism and the Western news media*. London: Sage.

Sperry, S. L. (1976). Television news as narrative. In R. Adler & D. Cater (Eds.), *Television as a cultural force* (pp. 129-146). New York: Praeger.

TV and the hostage crisis. (1985). *TV Guide*, September 21, pp. 6-25.

TV examines its excess. (1985). *Time*, July 22, p. 61.

Week in focus. (1985). *The Sunday Times*, August 4, pp. 17-18.

Weimann, G. (1987, Winter). Media events: The case of international terrorism. *Journal of Broadcasting and Electronic Media, 31*(1), 21-39.

8

The Myth of My Widow

A Dramatistic Analysis of News
Portrayals of a Terrorist Victim

JACK LULE

On October 7, 1985, on the Mediterranean Sea near Port Said, Egypt, four men hijacked the *Achille Lauro*, an Italian cruise ship, with 400 passengers and crew members aboard. The hijackers, identifying themselves as members of the Palestine Liberation Front, demanded the release of Palestinians imprisoned in several countries. They threatened to kill hostages if their demands were not met.

After two days of negotiations, the hijackers surrendered to Egyptian authorities. Soon after, Italian officials announced that an American tourist, Leon Klinghoffer, 69 years old and confined to a wheelchair, had been shot and his body thrown overboard during the hijacking. The United States demanded that the hijackers be prosecuted for the murder. On October 11, U.S. jets intercepted an Egyptian plane bound for Tunisia with the hijackers. The plane was forced to land at a NATO base in Italy, where the hijackers were charged with murder.

On October 14, a body washed ashore near the Syrian port of Tartus. On October 21, Leon Klinghoffer was buried in New Jersey.

For two weeks in October 1985, the *Achille Lauro* hijacking dominated U.S. news. It was a compelling news story with striking images

AUTHOR'S NOTE: Reprinted with permission from *Political Communication and Persuasion*, Vol. 5 (1988)

and action. Four hundred people were held hostage. Powerful political actors engaged in international negotiations. The story bristled with gripping moves, from the daring hijacking and brutal murder to the U.S. mid-air interception of a foreign jet.

Yet perhaps the most memorable image of the *Achille Lauro* hijacking was the face of Marilyn Klinghoffer. The widow of the victim received incredible international attention. She, rather than her husband, became the story. Reporters awaited her phone calls, in the Klinghoffers' New York apartment, with the couple's daughters, Lisa and Ilsa. Cameras followed Mrs. Klinghoffer as she left the *Achille Lauro* and as she arrived back in the United States. In the days after her arrival, news teams crowded the sidewalk outside her apartment. Her tears and faltering steps were recorded and replayed as she met her husband's body at Kennedy Airport. Her grief was broadcast worldwide on the day she buried him.

In the aftermath of the superabundance of news coverage, as the memory of the details of the hijacking fade but the power of the image of the widow remains, questions arise. How much coverage had the widow received? What was the nature of the coverage? Why was there such interest by the media in the Klinghoffer family, especially the widow? Why did the media probe most private moments of grief and mourning? Why was the story so compelling that the Klinghoffer family itself often willingly obliged the media? Why such terror and beauty in the story of the victim's widow? What can the stories say about terrorism and the news?

Some practical concerns of daily news can be acknowledged in partial explanation of the coverage of the widow and her family. Relatives are good sources for reporters. They have information about victims and often have had privileged contact with authorities. Relatives are convenient; they often are available to reporters; hijackers, hostages, and victims are not. Relatives can aid in "fleshing out" a story, giving human substance to unseen, far-off affairs, and providing deep, emotional content for complex, political stories.

Yet such pragmatic considerations pale beside the image of the widow and fail to capture or explain the intensity and real power of the news coverage. To suggest that Marilyn Klinghoffer was a good information source or supplied a feature angle does no justice to the drama and provides little understanding of the story. The news media responded to the terrorist killing of Leon Klinghoffer with a number of stories about his widow. The dramatic nature of those stories may provide insight into the complex relationship of terrorism and the news.

Drama and Myth

The drama of the story must be emphasized. Although it is commonplace for news stories to refer to terrorist incidents as "dramas," the reflexive implication—that the news story about terrorism is drama—often is not fully captured in such language.

Perhaps no modern writer has developed the implications of drama as much as Kenneth Burke (1941, 1966). In many works, he explored the concept of dramatism, an understanding of man as a symbol-using animal who acts in the world on the basis of meanings that symbols hold for him. For Burke, man is the only organism capable of action rather than motion. In this sense, drama is not a metaphor for action but a real description of human action. "In this sense," Burke (1976) wrote, "man is defined literally as an animal characterized by his special aptitude for 'symbolic action,' which is itself a literal term. And from there on, drama is employed, not as a metaphor but as a fixed form that helps us discover what the implication of the terms 'act' and 'person' really are" (p. 11).

With Burke's conception of dramatism, news can be studied as a symbolic act, the dramatic portrayal of a dramatic event. The study of news as drama, of course, was suggested in the writings of Walter Lippmann. News, Lippmann (1922) said, "is not a first hand report of the raw material. It is a report of that material after it has been stylized" (p. 347). News, he said, puts "pictures in our heads" (p. 3), simplified narratives that attempt to explain the complexities of events through drama. The philosopher George Herbert Mead (1934) also recognized the news as drama. "The vast importance of media of communication such as those involved in journalism is seen at once," he wrote, "since they report situations through which one can enter into the attitude and experience of other persons. The drama has served this function in presenting what have been felt to be important situations" (p. 257).

Historically, though, the dramas of experience, the simplified narratives of events, have been myths. Perhaps therefore, insight into particular news stories, such as the coverage of the widow of a terrorist victim, can be aided through a comparison of news and myth. What is meant by myth? The comparison will require a dynamic conception of myth, different from popular usage that refers to "myth" as an ancient, incredible tale or a demonstrably false story opposed to "reality." A more dynamic notion sees myth as an integral, unifying aspect of all cultures, ancient and modern. Writers who have worked with this notion of myth include Freud (1959), Jung (1959a), Cassirer (1946), and Malinowski (1954). For these writers, myth is a symbolic narrative that attempts to explain and give meaning to practices and beliefs. This conception is sensitive to the role of myth in ancient times but reflects a belief in the essentiality of myth within all cultures.

A mythic approach to news explores the news story as a symbolic narrative that attempts to give meaning to the events selected and described. A mythic approach might provide insight into the dramatic aspects of news stories about a terrorist victim. Faced with explaining the murder of a 69-year-old man in a wheelchair, journalists may have resorted, unconsciously or consciously, to myth. In turning to stories about the victim's widow, journalists may have resorted, unconsciously or consciously, to myth. In turning to stories about the victim's widow, journalists may have been drawn to powerful myths in an attempt to explain or give meaning to events that seemed beyond meaning.

Research in Terrorism, News, and Myth

In studying news stories about terrorism, the researcher is aided by a rapidly growing body of work in the academic and popular press. Two book-length studies summarize recent research and contain excellent bibliographies of the literature: *Terrorism, the media and the law,* edited by Abraham H. Miller (1982), and *Violence as communication,* by Alex P. Schmid and Janny de Graaf (1982). A more recent bibliography, which gives special attention to news, is the *Terrorism and the news media research bibliography,* compiled by Robert G. Picard and Rhonda S. Sheets (1986). Proceedings from a number of conferences on the media and terrorism also are of interest. These include *Terrorism and the media* and *Terrorism and the media in the 1980s,* both sponsored in part by the Institute for Studies in International

Terrorism (1977, 1983). The 1986 symposium report, Terrorism and the Media, published by the Overseas Press Club (1986) is an excellent, current source. Many articles in the academic press have been devoted to terrorism and the media. Of particular interest is a rhetorical study of terrorist coverage by Dowling (1986), a study of audience effects from terrorist press coverage by Weimann (1982), and a content analysis of differences in terrorist coverage between the *New York Times* and the London *Times* by Kelly and Mitchell (1981). The explosion of literature on terrorism and the media is evidence of the urgency of the topic and offers encouragement for further study.

A smaller but no less exciting array of work can be found devoted to news and myth. Among the noteworthy studies are a discussion by Sykes (1970) of how myth and news communicate abstract ideas in simple, concrete form; a study by Smith·(1979) of mythic narratives in television news; a mythic analysis of Canadian press coverage by Knight and Dean (1982), who show news media developing abstractions of expertise and legitimacy; and a discussion by Bennet (1980) of myth, ritual, and political communication. A monograph by Breen and Corcoran (1982), *Myth in the television discourse,* is of interest to this study. One of the functions of myth, the authors say, is to create models for society by translating one person's life history into an archetype for others. Later sections of this chapter will suggest that a similar process occurs within the media portrayal of the victim and his widow.

Three studies have applied mythic analyses to studies of news and terrorism. Lawrence and Timberg (1979) suggest that the selection and presentation of terrorist news coverage is strongly affected by myth. Davis and Walton (1983) find mythic aspects of consensus and closure in international coverage of the terrorist killing of Italian premier Aldo Moro. Paletz, Ayanian, and Fozzard (1982) conclude that mythic aspects of television news provide attention but not legitimation for terrorists.

It is of great interest that communication researchers have started to apply mythic analyses to the study of news and terrorism. Although still beginning, the exploration of mythic content and structure surely can add to understanding of the selection, presentation, and possible effects of news stories about terrorism. Through a mythic study of news portrayals of a victim of terrorism—portrayals that focused on the victim's widow—this chapter hopes to contribute to that important work.

The purpose of this chapter is to study, from the perspective of drama, an elite newspaper's coverage of the family of the terrorist victim, Leon Klinghoffer. The chapter will attempt to determine the amount of coverage given to the family. How much coverage did the widow receive, and what was the nature of the coverage? The chapter will study the dramatic aspects of the stories, including a categorization of acts, actors, settings, and themes. Using a definition of myth as a symbolic narrative that attempts to explain or give meaning to practices and beliefs, the chapter will offer a preliminary comparison of the news stories with myth. It will explore the possibility that the power and fascination of news stories about Leon Klinghoffer stemmed from highly dramatic portrayals of his widow, portrayals deeply rooted in myth. Finally, the chapter will consider the implications for public policy of possible mythic portrayals of terrorism in the news.

The microscopic nature of the study certainly is acknowledged; it isolates one aspect of one newspaper's coverage of one terrorist act. But in the attempt to probe beneath the surface of written accounts, interpretive research is forced to consider the minutiae of symbolic forms. Clifford Geertz (1973) says of interpretive studies: "The aim is to draw large conclusions from small, but very densely textured facts; to support broad assertions about the role of culture in the construction of collective life by engaging them exactly with complex specifics" (p. 28). Through the complex specifics of newspaper stories about a widow, this chapter hopes only to provide some consideration of possible mythic aspects of news coverage of terrorism, and to provide a ground for preliminary discussion of the implications of mythic portrayals of terrorism for public policy. It will address the following research questions:

(1) What was the extent of news coverage about the family and widow of Leon Klinghoffer? What was the location of such coverage in the paper? Did photographs accompany the coverage?

(2) From a dramatic perspective, what were the acts, actors, and settings of news coverage of the Klinghoffer family? What themes appear in the news stories?

(3) To what extent can the news stories be compared to myth, defined as a symbolic narrative that attempts to explain or give meaning to practices and beliefs? Do the news stories offer explanations for the murder

of Leon Klinghoffer? If so, in what ways? Do the news stories attempt to give meaning to the events? If so, in what ways?

(4) What might possible mythic portrayals say about the relationship between terrorism and the news? How might possible mythic portrayals of terrorism in the news affect public policy?

Drama as Method

New York Times stories were selected for study. Cited by Merrill (1968) as one of the world's elite newspapers, the *Times* is the most widely read paper within the U.S. government (Wess, 1974), and the most widely quoted newspaper (Gau, 1976). It is an invaluable paper for the study of U.S. news about international affairs. Besides these reasons of international influence, the *Times* is especially important for the dramatic considerations of this study because it is the "hometown" newspaper of the Klinghoffers, who lived on East 10th Street in Manhattan. The local angle of this otherwise international story provided the *Times* with great justification to cover the victim and his family. For example, a photo of the Klinghoffers, accompanying a story about local people held hostage on the *Achille Lauro*, appeared on the front page of the *Times* the day before the world learned of the murder.

The time period studied is October 8, 1985, to October 21, 1985. Although the hijacking took place over just two of these days, the story commanded coverage for two weeks because of the U.S. interception of the jet bearing the hijackers, and then the discovery and burial of Leon Klinghoffer's body.

The method of study is threefold. The first step is a content analysis of all *Times* stories related to the hijacking during the two-week period. For each day, the analysis notes the number of stories whose main subject was the Klinghoffer family, the page number of the story, and whether a photograph accompanied the story. The general theme of each news story, such as daughters' anxiety or widow's grief, is briefly noted.

With the basic accounting established of the amount of news coverage given the Klinghoffer family, the second method then analyzes each story, attempting to draw out its symbolic, dramatic aspects. The method is a dramatistic analysis, based on the work of Kenneth Burke. Although Burke can be read as a theoretician of drama, he was adamant that drama provided a methodological key to the study of symbolic action. "Dramatism is a method of analysis," Burke (1968) wrote, "and a corresponding critique of terminology designed to show that the most direct route to the study of human relations and human motives is via a methodological inquiry into cycles or clusters of terms and their functions" (p. 445). Burke's method begins by breaking down a story into its essential dramatic elements. These elements form a pentad: actors, acts, scenes, purposes, and agencies. Thus each news story about the Klinghoffers is examined through each element of the pentad.

Actors. The analysis isolates and identifies all characters in the news story. How is the individual actor described by the story? Does the actor appear to represent a larger entity such as a nation, religious group, government agency, or the public? Actors are also identified by predicate and function. What role does the actor play?

Act. Dramatism pays careful attention to the portrayal of action. The choice of words used to describe an individual action is studied. For example, the distinction is noted between *said* and *claimed,* or *killed* and *slaughtered.* The pattern of action within each news story—the plot—is examined for its logic and assumptions, origins and conclusions.

Scenes. The analysis notes the setting of the news story. How is the scene described by the story—friendly or forbidding, foreign or familiar? Does the scene play a role in the action? If so, in what way? Is the individual scene placed in a larger, global context?

Purposes. Dramatism studies the motivations and intentions of the actors. The analysis notes whether these purposes have been expressed by actors or offered by the news story. Does the story portray the purposes in positive, negative, or neutral terms, or not at all?

Agencies. The study examines the means, tools, and channels that the actors use to pursue their intentions. Are the agencies effective and successful? Does the news story portray the agencies in positive, negative, or neutral terms, or not at all?

Dramatistic analysis provides a means for the detailed consideration and categorization of the integral elements of a news story. It is an attempt to organize and make plain the structure and content of a text. It is particularly apt for news analysis. Besides its sensitivity to possible dramatic aspects in news, dramatism offers an intriguing comparison between the elements of the pentad and the traditional "five Ws and H": who, what, where, when, why, and how.

The organization of the dramatic elements of the story may also appear similar in approach to the structuralist "reconstruction" of a text (Barthes, 1957; Lévi-Strauss, 1967). But structuralists seek meaning not from outside the story but only from the relation of elements within the story. Burke would never deny the story a response to a situation or a world. Burke's analysis examines the latent content and structure of the text not to subsume the meaning of the individual story but to understand more fully the meaning of the individual story.

The third methodological step is the examination of patterns of portrayals among individual news stories. The categories of actors, acts, scenes, purposes, and agencies are studied for recurring images. No hunt for a fleeting reference in a forgotten paragraph, the analysis looks for obvious patterns among symbols and themes, what Hugh Duncan (1962) might call "the observable data of sociation, namely expressive symbols" (p. 146). It is here that the question of myth arises. The analysis asks the extent to which the patterns of portrayals in the news stories can be compared to myth, defined as a symbolic narrative that attempts to explain or give meaning to practices and beliefs. From the news stories of his family, can a narrative be found that attempts to explain or give meaning to the death of Leon Klinghoffer?

In summary, the chapter attempts to explore, in a preliminary fashion, possible mythic aspects of terrorist news coverage by examining news portrayals of the terrorist victim Leon Klinghoffer, concentrating particularly on stories about his family and widow. The story of the victim's widow is powerful and complex; the method of study combines traditional content analysis with dramatistic analysis in an attempt to examine fully the amount and nature of *New York Times* coverage of the widow. The chapter explores the possibility that news stories about Leon Klinghoffer focused on highly dramatic portrayals of his widow in an attempt to offer the comfort, order, meaning, and understanding of myth in response to the threat and challenge of terrorism.

Amount of News Coverage

In the first week of the hijacking, the *Times* devoted a small but consistent number of stories to the Klinghoffer family. The basic content analysis showed at least one story a day appeared in the *Times* about

Table 8.1 New York Times Stories About Leon Klinghoffer Family

Date	No. of stories	Page No.	Photo (page)	Theme
Oct. 8, 1985	—	—	—	—
Oct. 9	2	A1, A10	1 (A1)	daughters' anxiety
Oct. 10	1	A1, A10 A14	3 (A10, A14)	daughters' grief
Oct. 11	2	A1, A13 A1	1 (A1)	widow's grief/ victim as heroic/ victim as a loving man
Oct. 12	1	A8	—	victim as a happy man/ victim as a loving man
Oct. 13	4	A1, A24 A26	1 (A1)	widow's grief/ widow's rage/ widow's strength
Oct. 14	—	—	—	—
Oct. 15	—	—	—	—
Oct. 16	—	—	—	—
Oct. 17	—	—	1 (A1)	victim as hero
Oct. 18	—	—	1 (A10)	victim as hero
Oct. 19	—	—	—	—
Oct. 20	—	—	—	—
Oct. 21	1	A1, A6	1 (A1)	victim as symbol of good
Oct. 22	1	A10	1 (A10)	victim as symbol of good

the family. It has already been noted that a front-page story, with accompanying photograph, was published about the Klinghoffers on October 9, even before word of the killing. On October 13, when Marilyn Klinghoffer returned to the United States, four stories were devoted to her and her family.

Page numbers and accompanying photographs were noted in the analysis. As seen in Table 8.1, the page numbers and photographs suggest the prominence of the Klinghoffer stories in the *Times*. The Klinghoffer family appeared on the front page on four of the first seven days of the hijacking coverage. Mrs. Klinghoffer's photograph appeared on the front page of the *Times* three times, more than any other person that week.

Out of the many personalities involved in the events of that week —
personalities including the hijackers, the president of the United
States, the ship captain, and Leon Klinghoffer himself—it is of some
interest that the victim's widow received such prominence in the
Times.

Analysis of the second week of the hijacking coverage showed that
coverage of the Klinghoffer family dropped off sharply after the intense coverage of the widow's return to New York. Mrs. Klinghoffer
secluded herself in her apartment. With the remaining hostages freed
and the hijackers in custody, the *Achille Lauro* story was losing its
news interest. Even when a body washed ashore in Syria, and steps
were taken to identify the remains positively, the Klinghoffer family
was not mentioned in the *Times*. But when Mrs. Klinghoffer came out
of seclusion to receive her husband's body at the airport, she appeared
in a front-page story and photograph. On the following day,
accompanied by a mayor, governor, and two U.S. senators, the widow
buried her husband. And her slumped shoulders and wavering steps
were recorded by the *Times*.

The primary themes of the narratives, as seen in Table 8.1, reveal
the entire process of sorrow and grief captured by the *Times*. The initial anxiety of the daughters provided the theme for the first story.
The following day, anxiety gave way to horror and grief. When coverage settled upon Mrs. Klinghoffer, the story themes became the
mourning and then the eulogizing of her husband. These themes and
stories will be treated in more detail in the following section, but it is
important to note that the full chain of sorrow—from anxiety to burial—has been portrayed by the *Times*.

Table 8.2 summarizes the more descriptive, dramatistic analysis of
the news stories about the Klinghoffer family. The breakdown of each
story into its elements reveals the highly dramatic nature of the narratives. Primary characters always were the family members, the
widow and her daughters. Highly placed public officials, even President Ronald Reagan, were given minor roles in these stories.

The focus of the stories was the close depiction of grief, with little
emphasis on public and political aspects of events. Thus the acts—the
actions and plot—usually centered on a private, crucial moment:
word of death, return of the body, burial of the man. The scenes always heightened the intimacy of the act. The *Times* seemed to be present at the site and time of tragedy. In most stories about the

Table 8.2 Dramatistic Categorization of New York Times Stories About the Leon Klinghoffer Family

Date (#/stories)	Actors / Who	Act / What	Scene / When	Scene / Where	Purpose / Why	Agency / How
Oct. 9, 1985	two daughters	awaiting word	night before father's death	parents' apartment	anxiety, love, hopelessness	daughters tell stories; talk to reporters
Oct. 10	two daughters	receive word of father's death	the moment they receive word	parents' apartment	horror, grief	daughters scream; daughters observed
Oct. 11 (1)	widow	attempts to leave ship	as she leaves ship	Port Said, Egypt	despair	widow observed
Oct. 11 (2)	widow	tells daughters father a hero	widow's first phone call home	outside apartment	victim as hero	widow calls daughters; family tells reporters
Oct. 12	family	awaits widow & eulogizes victim	as family awaits widow	parents' apartment	victim as hero & loving man	relatives tell stories; talk to reporters
Oct. 13 (1)	widow	returns to U.S.	her return	airport	despair	widow observed
Oct. 13 (2)	widow	returns to U.S.	her return	airport	despair	widow observed
Oct. 13 (3)	widow	speaks to President	after return home	parents' apartment	widow's rage	widow tells President; family tells reporters
Oct. 13 (4)	widow	speaks to President	after return home	parents' apartment	widow's rage	widow tells President; family tells reporters
Oct. 21	widow	husband's body returned	as she meets the body	airport	victim as symbol of good	widow observed; politicians speak
Oct. 22	widow & family	burying victim	service & burial	synagogue & graveyard	victim as symbol of good	widow observed; rabbi speaks

Klinghoffers, a *Times* reporter was on the scene—in the living room of the apartment, at the *Achille Lauro*, at the airport, at the graveyard.

The purposes, intentions, and motivations of the actors were deeply personal and sharply drawn; through photographs and words, the anxiety, horror, sorrow, rage, and love of the Klinghoffers were made clear. The agencies—the channels by which actors voiced intentions or pursued purposes—were simple and sad expressions of human misery: the tears of a daughter dropping onto a photo album, or the hand of the widow touched to a flag-draped coffin. With each stark and terrible detail, the dramatistic analysis of the *Times* stories reveals the structure and the content of the narratives of grief.

Drama: Irony and Murder

On October 9, the Klinghoffers first appeared in the *New York Times*. A front-page story, headlined "To Hostage Families, Waiting Back Home Is Also a Nightmare," described the two daughters, Lisa and Ilsa, sitting by the telephone in their parents' Greenwich Village apartment. They had waited for news "all through the night Monday and all day Tuesday." Much family background was supplied. The daughters were particularly worried about their father, "who suffered a stroke several years ago that left him paralyzed on the right side and with slightly slurred speech." Despite his illness, Leon was a very active man, the daughters said, and he and his wife had greatly anticipated the cruise. They had celebrated their 36th wedding anniversary in September, and Lisa and Ilsa had given them luggage as a gift.

While they waited, the daughters tried "to comfort each other" with family jokes. "I can just picture Mommy telling Leon, 'Wait till we get back, they're not going to believe this,' "Ilsa told Lisa. The story ended with a quote from Ilsa's fiancé. "They're O.K.," he said. "They're O.K. I just know it!" Retrospect gives sad irony to the words. Retrospect also provides irony over the *Times'* choice to focus on this particular family to portray the anxiety of hostage relatives.

The next day's newspaper brought more drama: the death of Leon Klinghoffer. The lead story described the surrender of the hijackers and reported the killing of Klinghoffer. However, a second front-page story was devoted exclusively to an agonized, highly dramatic account of how the Klinghoffer family learned of the murder. Again, the *Times* reporter was on the scene, in the Greenwich Village apartment.

The story began with a celebration—daughters, relatives, and friends were lifting champagne glasses, "about to toast their parents' deliverance." Then the phone rang and the fiancé answered. Lisa and Ilsa, the reporter noted, "did not at first notice how quiet he became." He put the phone down and told the women their father might be dead. "Their screams, heartbreaking after so much jubilation, filled the living room where their friends and relatives looked at each other in horror and disbelief."

Drama, in this story, was created purposefully by the reporter. Because readers already were aware from the lead story and headlines that Klinghoffer was dead, the family story became a tragedy of discovery. The skill of the reporter must be noted, as well as the good news sense or "good fortune" that placed the reporter in the Klinghoffer apartment at that time. Also noted, however, might be what Hulteng (1976) calls the "uncomfortable voyeurism" (p. 164) into the lives of those thrust by tragedy into the news.

The dramatistic analysis makes note of patterns of portrayals. With the return on a second day to the actors and actions of the Klinghoffer family, a certain continuity of coverage was established. These people, even before the death of their loved one, had been chosen as a dramatic instrument. For the *Times*, the lead stories and reports on terrorism were not enough to convey the sense of the story. To interpret more meaningfully the chaotic events on the Mediterranean, the newspaper continued to follow the actions of the two young women waiting for their parents in New York. The next day, October 11, the news spotlight intensified on the Klinghoffers. No longer just one of the families affected by the *Achille Lauro* hijacking, the killing of Leon catapulted the family into international prominence. The *Times* ran two stories. On the front page, the scene had shifted to Port Said, Egypt, with a photograph of Marilyn Klinghoffer being escorted from the *Achille Lauro*. She was the face of tragedy. Her chin rested on her chest, and her eyes were sunk in dark circles. Her hair was windblown and wild. In sad contrast to her mourning, she still wore a bright, floral, low-necked dress from her holiday cruise.

The accompanying story on the front page referred to itself as "a vivid account" of the killing of Leon Klinghoffer, taken from interviews with passengers. Yet at the end, the focus returned to Mrs. Klinghoffer, as it recounted "the most moving scene" when the widow came ashore. "She was wearing a white flower print dress and was utterly downcast," the story read. "She barely raised her eyes to look at the mob of reporters and cameramen who pushed and shoved their way around her. Finally, Mrs. Klinghoffer, looking disraught [sic] looked up and said, 'Get away.' " A most moving scene? Authorities eventually had to take Mrs. Klinghoffer back to the ship—where her husband had been murdered—to escape the media mob on shore.

Suggestion of Myth: Victim as Hero

Another story that same day, October 11, developed an important theme that would continue to appear throughout the *Times* treatment of the Klinghoffer family. The theme was the portrayal of the victim as good, innocent, and heroic. The story was entitled, "Wife Calls Victim of Hijackers a Hero." It began with the words of the widow: " 'Your father was a hero,' Marilyn Klinghoffer told her two daughters yesterday." The story was partially devoted to the widow's "first telephone call home" since the hijacking, as related by Mrs. Klinghoffer's son-in-law. However, after giving a few details of the call, the story launched into the portrayal of a heroic, virtuous victim. Leon Klinghoffer was described as a "determined man" who fought hard to recover from his stroke. The son-in-law called him "a devoted husband, a loving father and a good friend." A friend said, "He was an unbelievably gentle man." A neighbor testified, "He always smiled, and he'd say hello." And a niece was quoted: "All he talked about was family and love."

It was here that the first outlines of myth might be seen. The suggestion of myth lay in a defined pattern of expressive symbols within the news stories. As seen in Tables 8.1 and 8.2, patterns did emerge. The *Times* coverage of the Klinghoffer family provided more than an intimate depiction of family grief. Within accounts about the widow, the *Times* wove portrayals of the victim as good and heroic. Using the drama of the widow's grief, the *Times* offered Leon Klinghoffer as a symbol of the innocent victim sacrificed.

On the following day, October 12, the *Times* continued to explore the dramatic, heroic portrayal of the victim. A long story was headlined, "Aged Victim, Portrayed as Helpless, Is Recalled as a Strong, Happy Man." Again, the *Times* appeared to be comfortably settled in the living room of the Klinghoffer apartment. Relatives have gathered, and they "looked at photographs of him and his wife Marilyn and the children, and they laughed at small memories." The story noted that on a coffee table in the middle of the room was a wedding photograph of the widow, "a beautiful, dark-haired young woman in a traditional wedding gown." Absent from the scene, on her way home to the United States, the widow was still placed by the story at center stage.

With this scene set, the *Times* then began the story of the victim's life, starting with the almost archetypal introduction for U.S. heroes: "He struggled all of his life . . . to overcome his humble beginnings on the Lower East Side." The story furnished more testimony as to the character and humanity of the victim. "He was a contented, happy man," his mother-in-law said. "He loved his friends and family." His daughter provided a glimpse of the man, recalling his fondness for the television show *Dynasty.* " 'He was addicted to *Dynasty,*'Lisa said. 'Joan Collins—wow!' "The story itself took an active, direct part in the testimony. "Everyone in the family went to Leon for advice," the story said, adding, "The entire family speaks of the courage with which Mr. Klinghoffer overcame two strokes several years ago."

The story also mentioned that President Reagan had telephoned and told the daughters that "their father was an American of whom everyone could be proud." An important dimension was added to the story with the inclusion of the president's words. By including the message, the story confirmed that the portrayal of Leon Klinghoffer as a heroic American was not solely a creation of the news story but was a view to be found in other areas of American public life. Dramatistic analysis of news must consider that news stories are symbolic expressions that create but also are created by culture.

The Widow

On Sunday, October 13, the *Times* coverage of the Klinghoffers climaxed with four stories—each centered upon the widow. Providing a graphic centerpiece for the narratives was a large, front-page photograph of Mrs. Klinghoffer arriving at Newark International Airport. The accompanying story described the scene: "Clad in black, staring straight ahead with a look of despair in her eyes," the widow was escorted to a limousine by two U.S. senators and a congressman—a reception befitting the widow of a hero.

Inside the paper, a second story provided another viewpoint of the widow's return home. This story contrasted the joy of other returning hostages with the gloom of Mrs. Klinghoffer. The others wore "cheerful pastel-colored cruise clothes;" the widow "wore a black shawl and black slacks." The other former hostages were united with relatives in a large, gay room filled with people; Mrs. Klinghoffer met her daughters in a private room. "In one room was jubilation, in the other grief. The doors were kept closed. This part of the homecoming was private."

Two other stories kept the focus of the *Times* on the widow. Both stories involved a telephone call from President Reagan to the widow. One was a transcript of the conversation, "as taken down by the Klinghoffer family and provided to the *New York Times*." The family's willingness to contribute to the public nature of the widow's grief was remarkable. A relative recorded the words of the widow and the president, and then immediately made these words available to the press. The public face to what might otherwise be a time of intimate mourning, reflected a kind of acknowledgment or acceptance by the family of the dramatic, public nature of the death of the victim.

A related story used the phone conversation between the president and the widow to talk about the widow's love for her husband and her rage at his killers. The story recounted a powerful moment in the phone conversation. "These people don't deserve to live. They are despicable," Mrs. Klinghoffer told the president. "No," the president replied. The widow told the president she faced the hijackers in a police lineup in Italy and that she "spit in their faces." The president answered, "You did. Oh God bless you." After this vignette, the story then depicted the strength and presence of the widow herself. Family members said that, "they were not just reassured, but awed, by the sight of her," the story reported. The fiancé said, " 'she's the bravest woman I've ever met.'" The story finished on a dramatic note "With Marilyn Klinghoffer home, the mourning of Leon Klinghoffer could now begin."

With five straight days of stories about the victim and his widow, culminating with four accounts in the Sunday paper about the widow, the *Times* provided a complex, detailed, and highly dramatic portrayal of grief in its first week of coverage of the hijacking and murder. Through almost microscopic examination of the love, anger, and pain of the widow, the news stories depicted the virtues of the victim. Through the appearance in the stories of public figures including senators, congressmen, and the president, the portrayal was acknowledged as a public phenomenon, with the victim transformed in the narratives into a national symbol of heroism and innocence. If myth is defined as a symbolic narrative that attempts to explain practices or beliefs, the week's news stories in the *Times* about Leon Klinghoffer and his widow might to some extent be compared to myth.

"He Will Live in His Nation's Memory"

In the next week, the *Times* coverage of the Klinghoffers dropped dramatically. Even when the body of Leon Klinghoffer was found, the family was not questioned or mentioned. The theme of the heroic victim might be seen, however, in two photographs. On October 17, a photograph of Klinghoffer's coffin, carried by Syrian soldiers, appeared on the front page of the *Times*. The front-page prominence given to the coffin, along with the military involvement, suggested that the victim was of international stature. The following day, a photograph of the Klinghoffers' daughters appeared in the newspaper. The women, continuing to maintain their public profile, held a press conference "announcing establishment of a fund to combat international terrorism in memory of Leon Klinghoffer."

On October 20, Leon Klinghoffer's body was returned to the United States. On October 21 and 22, the *Times* again devoted front-page scrutiny to the victim and his widow, and explicitly cited Klinghoffer as a national symbol of virtue and heroism. Accompanied by a front-page photograph of the widow and family standing beside the flag-covered coffin, the *Times* story, in its lead, made clear its symbolic intent: "While his widow wept, the mortal remains of Leon Klinghoffer were ceremoniously returned to his native city yesterday, and his memory was hailed by President Reagan and New York legislators as a symbol of innocence and goodness in a harsh world."

Within that one sentence, a number of the *Times'* dramatic portrayals and themes were neatly compressed. The sentence—the story—began with the focus trained on the widow. Before the president, before Leon Klinghoffer, the widow took the stage. "Mortal remains" suggested that other remains of the victim were immortal, which might refer to everlasting life or perhaps to the life of the victim in the nation's memory, both appropriate for a national hero. The presence in the story of the president and other legislators denoted the public stature of the victim, as did the reference to the ceremonious return. And finally, the victim was specifically hailed, by the officials and by the story, as a symbol of innocence and goodness; the symbolic narrative of the virtuous hero, of course, traditionally has been found in myth.

The body of the story continued to develop the same themes of goodness and heroism. Senator Daniel Patrick Moynihan called Klinghoffer "a symbol of righteousness in a world filled with evil and cruelty" and said the victim "will live in his nation's memory always for just those reasons." A statement from President Reagan proclaimed, "May Leon Klinghoffer's memory be a blessing to the world."

Through seven paragraphs, the story examined in minute detail the grief of the widow as she received her husband's body. "In dark glasses and a dark suit," she watched "impassively at first." Soon she "lifted her glasses and dabbed at her eyes." She "approached the coffin, put her hands to her lips and touched it." When the coffin was placed in the hearse, she "put her handkerchief to her face again." She was embraced and kissed by the dignitaries, and it "was then that she turned away and her body briefly sagged," but relatives supported her. Then, "escorted to a limousine, Mrs. Klinghoffer slumped bleak-faced in the rear seat."

Similar symbolic patterns—the heroic portrayal of the victim and the microscopic analysis of the widow's grief—appeared the following day in a *Times* story on the burial of Leon Klinghoffer. Headlined "Klinghoffer Eulogized as Public and Private Hero," the story followed the body from services at a synagogue to the ceremonies at the graveyard. The narrative again made explicit its symbolic thrust: "From a father, husband and small-appliance manufacturer who lived his 69 years, for the most part, in relative obscurity, Mr. Klinghoffer has been transformed into an international hero and political symbol."

With this story, two weeks of *Times* coverage of the Klinghoffers came to an end. As the newspaper itself noted, a once-unknown man had become an international hero and political symbol. In the *Times*, this transformation took place through the convergence of two patterns: the microscopic examination of the widow's grief, and the portrayal of the victim as an innocent, heroic man. Dramatistic analysis of the *Times* stories suggests that the news accounts can fruitfully be perceived as symbolic narratives that attempt to explain and give meaning to the events they portray. It has been suggested that, in this sense, the news stories might fruitfully be compared to myth. The following section will explore the notion of myth that might lie behind such stories, and discuss possible implications of mythic portrayals of terrorism for public policy.

Myth: The Sacrifice of the Hero

Through its stories on Leon Klinghoffer and his widow, the *Times* offered portrayals of the victim as a virtuous, heroic man who symbolized innocence and righteousness and whose death was cause for national mourning. Myth has been defined as a symbolic narrative that attempts to explain or give meaning to practices and beliefs, and the portrayals of Leon Klinghoffer, within the highly dramatic stories about his widow, certainly suggest the possibility of myth.

Indeed, the narrative of the death of the hero is one of the archetypal myths, found in cultures around the world. In "Ancient Myths and Modern Man," Joseph Henderson (Jung, 1964) writes, "Over and over again one hears a tale describing a hero's miraculous but humble birth," his proof of great strength, his battle with evil, "and his fall through betrayal or a 'heroic' sacrifice that ends in his death"(p. 101). In the *Times* stories focusing on his widow, Klinghoffer is the mythic hero, who "struggled all of his life . . . to overcome his humble beginnings." In death, Klinghoffer was "a hero," and "an American of whom everyone could be proud." He was a "symbol of innocence and goodness in a harsh world," and a "symbol of righteousness in a world filled with evil and cruelty."

In Western cultures, the symbolic narrative of the heroic, innocent victim sacrificed to evil finds its most perfect expression in the myth of Jesus Christ. (In this meaning, *myth* makes no judgment on the truth of a story; myth is a symbolic narrative that attempts to extend meaning). According to Carl Jung, the myth of Christ—the myth of the hero sacrificed—is of central importance to individuals. Jung (1959a) said that the compelling aspect of the myth is that the image "is a symbol of the self" (p. 367). He theorized that the symbol of Christ, as the hero, was so powerful in Western cultures that the symbol must exemplify the self (Jung, 1959b, p. 37). The thought was echoed by Jung's foremost disciple, Erich Neumann. In *The origins and history of consciousness*, Neumann (1970) states plainly that the hero is "the exemplar of individuality." (p. 380).

And so Leon Klinghoffer—portrayed within the myth of the sacrificed hero—becomes a symbol of the self in the pages of the *Times*. The myth may help explain the gripping nature of the media coverage of the terrorist victim and his family. From the words of the story may come the conscious or unconscious realization that the dramatic portrayal of the victim is the portrayal of the self. The myth of the hero has meaning, Henderson says (Jung, 1964), "both for the individual, who is endeavoring to discover and assert his personality, and for a whole society, which has an equal need to establish its collective identity." (p. 101) (Perhaps the myth also lies behind the terror of terrorism; the sacrificed hero could have been the self. In terrorism, the sacrificed hero is innocent of all but coincidence.)

It is the demands of this mythic portrayal of the self that might explain the minute, dramatic depiction of the widow's grief within the news stories. Every bit of grounding, every device used to locate the victim as a real person in a specific time and place, better serves to portray him as an individual and exemplar of the self. And so the stories detail his humble beginnings, his job selling small appliances, his marriage, his battle to overcome strokes, his fondness for *Dynasty* and Joan Collins. And the stories examine each movement of the widow's grief: the handkerchief to the eye, the hand to the lip and then the coffin, the sag of her body, and the slump of her shoulders. This sacrifice is no fiction, one thinks; the victim is a real person and it could have been *my-self*.

In their symbolic transformation of events to myth, of victim to self, the news stories build a detailed portrayal not unlike James Joyce's novel *Ulysses*. The book is crammed with the staggering details of Leopold Bloom's life until finally, the details collapse, and Bloom is revealed as the hero Ulysses, and Ulysses is revealed as the symbol of the self. In the same way, the *Times* stories provide details about the Klinghoffer family. "The nature of the hero is as manifold as the agonizing situations of real life," Neumann writes (1970, p. 378). "But always he is compelled to sacrifice normal living in whatever form it may touch him, whether it be mother, father, child, homeland, sweetheart, brother or friend."

The myth of the hero may also work with the examination of the grief of the widow to add another compelling aspect to the narratives. For if indeed the sacrificed hero is *my-self*, then the news allows me the privileged opportunity to attend my own death. The age-old question can be answered: What will it be like when I die? In a real way, through the myth of the hero and the symbol of the self, I can view the effect of my death and the testimony of my life. I see the grief of my widow as she touches my coffin and staggers in grief. My family and friends mourn my passing; I'm curious—who showed up? I share the outrage of the world that my life should have been cut short. Clergy, senators, even the president testify to my worth; I was a symbol of righteousness, a blessing to the world. Even in the face of the meaninglessness of life that must end in death, symbolized so well by my meaningless victimage to terrorism, I can see that my life had meaning after all.

Faced with giving meaning to the murder of Leon Klinghoffer, faced with giving meaning to life in the face of death, the news stories have appealed to the power of myth. Perhaps only myth is capable of balancing the eternal opposition—what Freud (1961) called the "battle of the giants":

> And now, I think, the meaning of the evolution of civilization is no longer obscure to us. It must present the struggle between Eros and Death, between the instinct of life and the instinct of destruction, as it works itself out in the human species. This struggle is what all life essentially consists of, and the evolution of civilization may therefore be simply described as the struggle for life of the human species.

Life and death struggle in the news stories. Invoking the great myth of the hero, the news stories seek to answer the terrorist negation that they report. Terrorism offers death, but the news stories offer life. Terrorism has said the self is meaningless, but the news stories of the hero's widow affirm that the self has meaning.

Implications: Myth, Terrorism, and Public Policy

Dramatistic analysis has suggested that the *New York Times* portrayals of the terrorist killing of Leon Klinghoffer may contain a mythic dimension. Although the study has been quite small in scope and exploratory in approach, it may be beneficial to at least consider possible implications of mythic news portrayals of terrorist victims.

A primary implication already has been alluded to. Through the myth of the hero, the news stories invoked the symbol of the self, inviting intense identification of the individual reader with the terrorist victim. But in doing so, the news stories also provided the terror of terrorism. As a symbolic expression, terrorism is an act of communication between the terrorists and an audience, which might be an individual, a nation, or a world. Much of the power of the terrorist statement lies in its symbolic aspects. Often unknown by their killers, the terrorist victims are meant to represent symbolically a nation, a religion, or an institution. The terror—opposed to disgust over the slaughter, or grief over the loss—resides in the personal realization that the victim is a symbol of the self as member of a nation or institution. Only coincidence, fate, timing, or happenstance places that particular member in the hands of the terrorist at that time. It could have been *my-self*, the symbol says.

The news stories that drew from the myth of the hero, that invoked the symbol of the self in response to terrorism, thus helped the terrorists establish the link between the victim and the self. On the surface level, the news accounts of the victim's widow informed the public of the circumstances and effects of the terrorist act. The violence and the sadness made for compelling reading. But on a deeper level, the mythic tale of the hero who was sacrificed to evil did much more than inform. The news stories invited intense identification of the reader with the victim, allowing real communication between the terrorist and individual members of the community. To the extent that media portrayals of terrorist victims continue to invoke the myth of the hero, especially through the powerful dramatization of family grief, the ability of terrorists to communicate with the community should remain strong.

The symbolism of terrorism was also aided by the actions of public officials portrayed in the media. The involvement of public officials with Marilyn Klinghoffer explicitly affirmed the myth of the hero portrayed in the media. The victim was the terrorists' symbol of the nation, and was so honored by the media and mourned by officials. Actions of the government figures, portrayed by the media, thus also helped the terrorists establish symbolic expression with the national community. The recognition of the victim on national terms by public officials confirmed the symbolic aspect of the terrorist message.

However, policymakers may not always be mere pawns, reacting to terrorist manipulation. Without appearing too cynical, it is pertinent to note that acceptance of the mythic portrayal of the victim as hero allows politicians access to the media. For example, acceptance of the myth allowed politicians access to the power and drama surrounding the grief of Marilyn Klinghoffer. Much political gain might have been realized through embracing the widow on a public stage. (Conversely, it should also be noted that the media certainly benefited from the public interest in the dramatic stories of the victim and his widow. Mythic portrayals of terrorism may be a good example of the ways in which the media create and are also created by culture.)

Other political implications from news portrayals of the myth of the hero, and the mourning of the victim as a symbol of a nation or community, might be suggested. Policymakers can appeal to the power of the myth to arouse support for measures of prevention and reprisal. For example, restrictions on travel by U.S. citizens to areas of the Middle East were preventive measures based on perceived dangers faced by individual U.S. citizens. The restrictions recognized the symbolism of terrorism—each individual was qualified to serve as a symbol of the nation for terrorists.

Mythic images in the news might also help public officials create a powerful climate for revenge. An attack against an individual citizen can be recognized by the media, politicians, and the public as an attack against the nation. For example, on April 14, 1986, U.S. air and naval forces bombed Libya. In a speech that night, President Reagan (1986) said the attack was a direct response to terrorism against U.S. citizens. "I warned Colonel Khadafy that we would hold his regime accountable for any new terrorist attacks launched against American citizens," the president said. "When our citizens are abused or attacked anywhere in the world on the direct orders of a hostile regime, we will respond so long as I'm in this Oval Office." Without considering the wisdom of the bombings or the possible "effects" of news stories, it can at least be suggested that mythic portrayals of terrorist victims in the news might help create or sustain a climate that allows the bombing of a city in response to the taking of an American life.

The microscopic approach of this study prevents any attempt at linking news coverage to aspects of social life. The nature of the study also prohibits generalizing from its analysis to other newspapers or to other terrorist incidents. Much preliminary work needs to be done on the relationship among the media, terrorism, and myth, and their relation to public policy. This study hopes at least to offer consideration of possible mythic portrayals of terrorism in the news. Perhaps news stories not only provide information on terrorism to a society but also, through the dramatic portrayal of symbols, give meaning to that society's practices and beliefs. Perhaps then, in such situations, news can be read as myth.

References

Barthes, R. (1957). *Mythologies* (A. Lavers, Trans.). London: Jonathan Cape.

Bennet, W. (1980, Autumn). Myth, ritual and political control. *Journal of Communication, 30*, 166-179.

Breen, M., & Corcoran, F. (1982, June). Myth in the television discourse. *Communication Monographs, 49*, 127-136.

Burke, K. (1941). *The philosophy of literary form.* Baton Rouge: Louisiana State University Press.

Burke, K. (1966). *Language as symbolic action.* Berkeley: University of California Press.

Burke, K. (1968). Dramatism. In D. Sills (Ed.), *The international encyclopedia of the social sciences, Vol. 7* (pp. 445-451). New York: Macmillan.

Burke, K. (1976). Dramatism. In J. Combs & M. Mansfield (Eds.), *Drama in life* (pp. 7-17). New York: Hastings House.

Cassirer, E. (1946). *The myth of the state.* New Haven, CT: Yale University Press.

Davis, H., & Walton, P. (1983). Death of a premier. In H. Davis & P. Walton (Eds.), *Language, image, media* (pp. 8-50). New York: St. Martin's.

Dowling, R. (1986, Winter). Terrorism and the media: A rhetorical genre. *Journal of Communication, 35*,(1), 12-24.

Duncan, H. (1962). *Communication and social order.* New York: Oxford University Press.

Freud, S. (1959). Writers and day-dreaming. In J. Strachey (Ed. & Trans.), *The standard edition of the complete psychological works of Sigmund Freud* (Vol. 10). London: Hogarth.

Freud, S. (1961). Civilization and its discontents. In J. Strachey (Ed. & Trans.), *The standard edition of the complete psychological works of Sigmund Freud,* (Vol. 21). London: Hogarth.

Gau, C. (1976). What publications are most frequently cited in the *Congressional Record*? *Journalism Quarterly, 53*, 716-719.

Geertz, C. (1973). *The interpretation of cultures.* New York: Basic Books.

Henderson. J. (1964). Ancient myths and modern man. In C. Jung (Ed.), *Man and his symbols* (pp. 95-156). New York: Dell.

Hulteng, J. (1976). *The messenger's motives.* Englewood Cliffs, NJ: Prentice-Hall.

Institute for Studies in International Terrorism. (1977). *Terrorism and the media* [Conference proceedings]. New York: Author.

Institute for Studies in International Terrorism. (1983). *Terrorism and the media in the 1980s* [Conference proceedings]. New York: Author.

Jung, C. (1959a). *The archetypes and the collective unconscious.* New York: Pantheon.

Jung, C. (1959b). *AION.* New York: Pantheon.

Jung, C. (1964). *Man and his symbols.* New York: Dell.

Kelly, M., & Mitchell, T. (1981). Transnational terrorism and the western elite press. *Political Communication and Persuasion, 1*, 69-96.

Knight, G., & Dean, T. (1982, Spring). Myth and the structure of news. *Journal of Communication, 32*, 144-158.

Lawrence, J., & Timberg, B. (1979, Summer). News and mythic selectivity. *Journal of American Culture, 2*, 321-330.

Lévi-Strauss, C. (1967). *Structural anthropology* (C. Jacobson & B. Schoef, Trans.). Garden City, NY: Anchor-Doubleday.

Lippmann, W. (1922). *Public opinion*. New York: Macmillan.

Malinowski, B. (1954). *Myth in primitive psychology: Magic, science and religion and other essays*. Garden City, NY: Doubleday.

Mead, G. (1934). *Mind, self, and society*. Chicago: University of Chicago Press.

Merrill, J. (1968). *The elite press*. New York: Pitman.

Miller, A. H. (Ed.). (1982). *Terrorism, the media and the law*. Dobbs Ferry, NY: Transnational.

Neumann, E. (1970). *The origins and history of consciousness* (R. Hull, Trans.). Princeton, NJ: Princeton University Press.

Overseas Press Club. (1986). *Terrorism and the media*. [Symposium Report]. New York: Author.

Paletz, D., Ayanian, J., & Fozzard, P. (1982). Terrorism on TV news. In W. Adams (Ed.), *Television coverage of international affairs* (pp. 143-165). Norwood, NJ: Ablex.

Picard, R., & Sheets, R. (1986). *Terrorism and the news media research bibliography*. Columbia, SC: Association for Education in Journalism and Mass Communication.

Reagan, R. (1986). Televised speech. [Text] *Atlanta Constitution*, April 15, p. 6A.

Schmid, A., & de Graaf, J. (1982). *Violence as communication*. Beverly Hills: Sage.

Smith, R. (1979, Winter). Mythic elements in television news. *Journal of Communication, 29*, 75-82.

Sykes, A. (1970, March). Myth in communication. *Journal of Communication, 20*, 17-31.

Weimann, G. (1982, Winter). The theater of terror: Effects of press coverage. *Journal of Communication, 33*, 38-46.

Weiss, C. (1974). What America's leaders read. *Public Opinion Quarterly, 38*, 1-22.

9

The Literature of Terrorism

Implications for Visual Communications

KEVIN G. BARNHURST

The literature of terrorism has grown dramatically since the issue began receiving academic attention in the last quarter century. Terrorism is universally defined in the literature as a form of violence or violent threat (Schmid & Jongman, 1988). It is overgeneralizing only slightly to say that the central issue in the literature of terrorism is the assigning of responsibility for the phenomenon. This issue is not surprising given the pejorative connotations of the term that defines the field. *Terrorist* is not a neutral word, and calling any individual or group by that name assigns some degree of guilt (Knauss & Strickland, 1988, p. 91).

Applying the term to governments has led to a distinction between official types of conduct. Violence used to enforce laws and wage war is not usually considered terrorism, but extralegal violence perpetrated by the state or its supporters falls into the special category of state terrorism (Schmid & de Graaf, 1982, p. 60). The negative force of the term condemns this special case of violence while distinguishing it from the ordinary sense of the term, which is reserved for other groups and for individuals.

Much of the literature dwells on the question of why these persons act, in an attempt to justify, excuse, condemn, or explain their violence. Many disciplines contribute to the flood of writing on the topic (Bell, 1978, pp. 280-285; Schmid & Jongman, 1988). Each attempts to explain the phenomenon from its particular perspective. Common crimes are not considered terrorism unless they are committed for political ends, and political scientists have proposed two types of explanations for the violent means to those ends. One, based on the political discourse of terrorists themselves, provides a variety of individual rationales for violence (Schmid & Jongman, 1988, pp. 79-86). Another proposes that terrorists act because they are otherwise excluded from political life. This proposition is built on the concept of "relative deprivation" (Gurr, 1970, pp. 3-4), a contribution that came by way of psychoanalysis and suggests that "misery, frustration, grievance, and despair" motivate terrorists (United Nations Secretariat, 1975, p. 10).

The political and rational nature of terrorism distinguishes it from the acts of lunatics. Psychologists suggest that peace is the norm for human behavior and that terrorists are deviant personalities (Schmid & Jongman, 1988, p. 87). The fear they produce draws force from their involvement in groups, and other scholars have examined this aspect. Terrorism is generally viewed as organized and systematic, one event containing the promise of more to come. Military scientists consider terrorism a form of surrogate war (p. 98), and sociologists have proposed that terrorism is a part of the normal level of aggressive behavior in societies that lack alternative modes of social change (p. 111). Finally, the victims of terrorism, whether they are killed, held hostage, or deprived of property, are broadly held to be innocent.

Because contemporary terrorism often involves the media, communications scholars have also contributed to the literature of terrorism (Picard & Sheets, 1986). The news media report on violence of all kinds—domestic and public violence of criminals and the police, mass murder by madmen, and civil and foreign wars, as well as terrorism. Many of the violent thrive on secrecy, but some criminals find advantage in making the news, either to gain personal notoriety or to forward their political aims. News of violence has value to individuals, businesses, and governments, which construct a view of society and make decisions based on its presence or likelihood. And of course it has value to the media in a variety of ways, most obviously when it increases the audience (Galtung & Ruge, 1970, pp. 259-298). Big news events get heavy coverage and attract public attention. When coverage is a political goal of the violent, the media are often accused of collusion.

The confluence of motives among the media, the public, and terrorists is at the heart of the debate over terrorism and the media. Much of the literature of the field is general in nature—essays and articles by scholars and media professionals who attempt to explain terrorism and its relationship with the media using logical argument. They cite anecdotal evidence, for the most part, but some quantitative studies have been undertaken to verify or challenge the assumptions in the essays.

Like much of the literature, media scholarship seeks to assign responsibility for terrorism and simultaneously to explain why the violence occurs. The argument goes something like this: When the media give heavy play to a story of terrorism, in order to serve the audience, they unwittingly forward the purposes of the terrorists. The charges of media collusion usually condemn specific forms, such as the size of newspaper headlines or the extent of television coverage. These qualities are, at their core, visual. They are questions of relative space and scale over time. Yet scholars of visual communications have not yet turned their attention to terrorism.

This chapter is divided into two parts. The first examines the general literature of terrorism and the media, laying out its arguments and identifying its major questions. This description will necessarily be cursory, but it will rely to the degree possible on the literature itself so that visual communications scholars may read some of the original argument firsthand and identify major sources in the field. The first section concludes with a summary of the literature. The second part of the chapter then examines all the available studies of terrorism for a single medium, the newspaper. An exhaustive survey of a single type of media demonstrates the state of thought and methodology in the field and may be useful to scholars who wish to examine other media. The studies are described in some detail, to identify the issues and the methods of interest to visual researchers. In the absence so far of similar work by visual communications specialists, these studies form a foundation upon which visual research may build. The chapter concludes by suggesting some implications for visual communications scholarship in the future.

Part 1: Terrorism and the Media

Expert opinion on terrorism and the media can be crudely divided into two schools. The great majority of authorities consider the media culpable to some degree for terrorism. Their writing has spawned a variety of hypotheses to describe the instrumental role of the media. A scattered few take issue, arguing that the media are vulnerable to but not responsible for terrorism. The prescriptions for solving the problem range from a policy of laissez-faire to a call for outright censorship.

Culpable Media

Some authors assert that the media can cause or increase terrorism. Yonah Alexander, editor of the journal *Terrorism*, suggests that "extensive coverage by the media is a major reward for terrorists. . . . Reporting on terrorism increases the effectiveness of its message through repetition and imitation" (Midgley & Rice, 1984, p. 2). Citing anecdotes about the assassinations of Presidents McKinley and Kennedy, Alex P. Schmid and Janny de Graaf (1982) in their book *Violence as communication* argue that reporting terrorism is likely to increase terrorist activities: "Without communication there can be no terrorism" (pp. 140, 170). In an earlier essay, Alexander (1979, pp. 162-166) enumerated the ways in which such reporting influences the public: increasing awareness of terrorist groups; exporting violent techniques to other individuals or groups, which "triggers similar extreme actions"; and exacerbating terrorist acts by interfering with police operations and increasing pressure on authorities or by harassing relatives or survivors. These three effects can be called the awareness, contagion, and interference hypotheses.

Interference

Interference may involve direct physical involvement in an event, such as a reporter mediating between terrorists and police, or indirect pressure on officials to end the violence or threat. Support for this hypothesis comes from anecdotes told by police and others involved in hostage cases (Rabe, 1979, p. 69). Robert G. Picard (1986, p. 148), a director of the terrorism research project for the Association for Education in Journalism and Mass Communication, also suggests that heavy media coverage affects government decision making. There can be little doubt that reporters inconvenience the authorities in some cases, but the problem is not by any means peculiar to incidents of terrorism. The issue might be better handled as a special case in the context of media and government relations.

The interference hypothesis does point up an important source of confusion. Frequently authorities do not distinguish between the effects of print and electronic media coverage. For example, one writer states that "acts of terrorism will be instantly publicized by the television, radio, and press" (Wilkinson, 1978, pp. 4-5; 1986, p. 103). Newspapers are far from instant in their coverage. Description, quotation, and still photography—the ingredients of newspapers—are more filtered than live television coverage. Journalists recognize these differences more often than do academics. Franco Salomone (1975) of *Il Tempo di Roma* in Italy says, "The perpetrators of [terrorist] acts rely less on printed coverage for publicity because it is slower and reaches a smaller audience" (p. 44).

Broadcast news, by time constraint and custom, tends to be less explanatory than printed news. Action footage and sound—the ingredients of broadcast coverage—are less filtered than print coverage and are more likely to have an immediate impact. In a symposium held July 24, 1984, at the Second Conference on International Terrorism in Washington, DC, several panelists singled out television. Daniel Schorr said, "Media terrorism is primarily a television problem" (Terrorism and the media, 1984, p. 53).

The two media forms also differ in their general approach to violence (Gerbner, 1988). A study by the Ontario Ministry of Government Services in 1977 found that television dedicated a larger share of its total coverage to violence and conflict than did newspapers. The share of coverage on television emphasized actual or threatened violence, whereas the share of coverage in newspapers emphasized items on conflict, a category that is more general and vague by nature (Ontario Royal Commission, 1977, pp. 603-604). The differences between the media are significant enough that investigation of the two ought, at least initially, to be conducted separately (see Chapter 6).

Contagion

The term *contagion*, as used by Michael J. Kelly and Thomas H. Mitchell (1981, p. 274) in their study, implies that terrorism spreads, sometimes by other means but most often through the media. Wilkinson (1986, p. 210) cites nonmedia examples of terrorist groups holding conferences that have a "bandwagon effect." The contagion hypothesis was described most pointedly by Schmid and de Graaf (1982): "Epidemic diseases like malaria have been successfully fought by killing the disease-carrying mosquito. Epidemics of nonstate terrorism are spread mainly by the modern mass media. The implication seems obvious" (p. 148).

Although they label it a "simplistic line of reasoning" followed by governments, Schmid and de Graaf support the thesis. They cite the example of the Tupamaro guerrillas in Uruguay, who were "widely reported" to "have offered an example to countless terrorist movements abroad" (p. 24). They also offer this historic example from newspapers:

> Fascinated by those anarchists who proudly accepted responsibility for their political crimes, the late nineteenth-century press gave ample space to terrorist deeds and thereby probably contributed to the spread of this new style of political confrontation. (Gerbner et al., 1978, pp.176-207; Schmid & de Graaf, 1982, p. 14.)

Support for the contagion hypothesis is anecdotal and speculative. Picard (see Chapter 5) decries the absence of data, concluding that not a single study based on accepted social science research methods has established a cause-effect relationship between media coverage and the spread of terrorism.

The contagion hypothesis not only blames the media but contains a remedy for terrorism, which will be discussed in a subsequent section on prescriptions.

Awareness

The diffusion concept of mass media would seem to support the idea that media coverage increases public awareness of terrorism (see Chapter 5). Gabriel Weimann (1983) examined the effects of reading press clippings about two hijackings (one of an airplane, the other of a train) in 1975 and 1976 on attitudes toward terrorists: "Students who were exposed to media coverage of a terrorist event tended to consider the event more important and noteworthy and to call for a solution" (p. 44).

Opinion differs on whether increased awareness in itself is problematic. Weimann's research supports the idea of Lazarsfeld and Merton (1948, pp. 95-118) that the media perform a "status conferral function." This circular argument—that if you matter you're covered in the media, and if you're in the media, you matter—is forwarded by several authors (Terrorism and the media, 1984, p. 53; Wilkinson, 1978, p. 2) and is part of the recent return of the concept that the mass media are powerful (Weimann, 1983, p. 39). Viewing the media as powerful and effective leads to two conclusions: that the media are likely to spread terror and, therefore, that they ought to be controlled in some way.

Vulnerable Media

A few writers from diverse quarters oppose placing blame on the media. They instead support the view that the media are victims of terrorism. Paul Wilkinson (1978), senior lecturer in politics at University College, Cardiff, Canada, argues that "the ruthless bargaining in human lives, typical of any terrorist action, does not depend upon the existence of mass media" (p. 2). Brian Jenkins (1983), director of the Security and Subnational Conflicts Program at the Rand Corporation, says that "mass communication is responsible for terrorism to about the same extent that civil aviation is responsible for hijackings" (p. 171). And journalist Bernard Johnpoll (1977) suggests:

> It is useless to discuss what the media can do about terror. The media are not judicial institutions; their sole role in modern society is to transmit information. How to erase terror is a juridical and ethical question, not a question of the media. (pp. 159-160)

These assertions require little elaboration. They essentially argue for the absence of a phenomenon. In a seminar sponsored by two Chicago newspapers, M. Cherif Bassiouni, a DePaul University law professor, said he could find no reason to blame the media: "We are speculating about the correlation between media coverage and terrorism. It's a speculation on which we have, really, no hard data" (The media and terrorism, 1977, p. 36). Citing the lack of evidence is not a timid or tentative position in the debate; it presents a concrete challenge to the culpable-media camp, which has responded by disparaging the argument (Schmid & de Graaf, 1982, p. 143). The disagreement over responsibility identifies a central difficulty in the study of terrorism and the media: the burden to establish proof that the media are guilty of spreading or exacerbating terror.

News Play

Although writers do not agree on whether the media cause terrorism, they almost universally condemn the treatment of terrorist events. The historian Walter Laqueur (1977) asserts, "The media, with their inbuilt tendency toward sensationalism, have always magnified terrorist exploits quite irrespective of their intrinsic importance" (p. 109). Schmid and de Graaf (1982) suggest that there have been many examples "where the media squeezed the most out of a relatively minor terrorist incident" (p. 78). Robert L. Rabe (1979), assistant chief of police, Metropolitan Police Department, Washington, DC, says, "it is not the presentation of such news that gives rise to concern, but the manner in which it is presented" (p. 69).

The form of presentation is especially important in newspapers. Schmid and de Graaf (1982, p. 14) criticize the amount of space dedicated to terrorism coverage (also see Gerbner et al., 1987, pp. 176-207). Wilkinson (1986, p. 60) specifically cites the problem of big headlines and identifies "a kind of Gresham's Law of Terror: 'those who spill the most blood win the biggest headlines' " (Wilkinson, 1978, p. 3). The charge of exaggerated news play tends to be specific to the form of news: Broadcasting is criticized for live coverage and its duration, and the press for visually prominent and extensive coverage of terrorism. Although writers seem to cite specific aspects of form, their indictments are ultimately vague from the perspective of visual communications. They do not propose concrete differences between routine and exaggerated coverage either in length or in, say, the use of pictures or color. They offer no evidence beyond the simple assertion that prominent news play emphasizes certain aspects of the form of news presentation.

Nor do these formal aspects address the judgment of newspaper journalists that the coverage is appropriate to the events. John O'Sullivan, a columnist for the London *Daily Telegraph*, approves of the prominent coverage in popular tabloids: "I suggest that the reporting on terrorism in the so-called popular press is much more accurate than it is in the more serious newspapers" (Terrorism and the media, 1984, p. 54). Editors may play up a story because it merits emphasis. Salomone (1975) argues that "it is not the coverage which is sensational as much as the news" (p. 43). None of the writers attempts to draw a useful distinction between coverage that merely reflects the events and news play that exaggerates events.

Prescriptions

Most authorities find fault with the way news is presented, whether they consider the media culpable or not, and they usually suggest some sort of intervention. There is considerable crossing of lines between the two schools of thought. An author who believes the media are victimized, for example, might recommend internal guidelines to reduce their vulnerability. Nevertheless, the prescriptions tend to follow from the writers' initial position on the question of media responsibility.

Those who argue that the media contribute to terrorism almost invariably call for some type of intervention. There are many forms of media control. Some are codified in rules and procedures of government and the media; others are tacit, embedded in the culture of media professions. Some operate directly; others are indirect. In line with the general character of the literature of terrorism and the media, authorities tend to dismiss the nuances of the terms and group all forms of intervention according to their origins within either government or the media. As a result they discuss two broad possibilities, censorship and self-restraint.

Censorship

"The inherent right of the public to be informed is somewhat limited by another public interest—that of denying terrorists the means to communicate their message of propaganda and instill in the public the element of fear so necessary to their operation," argues Rabe (1979, p. 68). In 1977, UN Ambassador Andrew Young called for legal restrictions on the coverage of violent crimes (Terrorism and fit news, 1977, p. 36). O'Sullivan supported the ban on IRA interviews (Terrorism and the media, 1984, p. 53). Schmid and de Graaf (1982) argue that newspapers should face legal sanctions: "The press should, in our view, be held responsible for media-made disasters just as individuals are held responsible for man-made disasters" (p. 147). They do not specify just how this proposal might be carried out.

Most observers condemn censorship, although they use the absence of terrorist acts in the Soviet Union as proof that the media cause terrorism. Jenkins (1983) says, "It is interesting to note that very little terrorism is seen in totalitarian countries, leading some to consider the possibility that terrorism is a product of freedom, particularly of the freedom of the press" (p. 160). Nicholas Ashford, Washington bureau chief for the London *Times*, says that "any attempts to curb media coverage of terrorist activities must be seen as a form of political censorship" (Midgley & Rice, 1984, p. 42).

There are several arguments against censorship: that it is unenforceable, escalates the violence, causes political instability, and erodes the public trust in the media. Ashford asserts, "Curbs on press coverage . . . would be almost impossible to enforce" (p. 43). Alexander (1979) argues that "any attempts to impose media blackouts are likely to force terrorists to escalate the levels of violence in order to attract more attention" (p. 170). He also advocates accurate reporting of terrorist acts "lest the public panic and lose trust and confidence in both the press and the government" (p. 170). Rabe (1979) says, "Imposing a partial or total news blackout is both idealistic and counterproductive. It would have the effect of masking from the people the reality of some of the problems this country faces" (p. 70). And H. H. A. Cooper (1977) argues that

> suppression of the event, which could hardly be attained in its entirety, might well, through partial revelations, halftruths, and frightening speculations, be a greater mischief. Confidence in the media would certainly be lost and authority itself called into question. The terrorist would have succeeded, incidentally, in causing that very crisis of creditability [sic] that is an important secondary objective of his war on society. (pp. 151-152)

Guidelines

Some form of self-control is preferred by a majority of observers, including scholars, government experts, and journalists. Stephen S. Rosenfeld (1975), writing on the editorial pages of the *Washington Post*, said:

> We of the Western press have yet to come to terms with international terror. If we thought about it more and understood its essence, we would probably

stop writing about it, or we would write about it with a great deal more restraint. (p. A19)

Wilkinson (1978) argues that "the proper way to do this in a democracy is to encourage the mass media to develop and enforce their own voluntary guidelines and self-restraint in terrorism coverage" (p. 177). Daniel Schorr says, "I suggest that we in the news business impose some voluntary limits" (Terrorism and the media, 1984, p. 53). Bassiouni (1981, pp. 1-51; 1982, pp. 128-143) drew the same conclusion in his study for the U.S. Law Enforcement Assistance Administration.

Stick to facts. One guideline most frequently suggested is that the media give "just the facts." Robert H. Kupperman (1979), chief scientist with the U.S. Arms Control and Disarmament Agency, suggests:

> The news must be reported, but a code of ethics should arise from within the media. . . . Ideally, if the media could underplay the terrorist event and yet report the facts, we could go a long way toward ritualizing a lesser theatrical production and thus keep terrorism within bounds. (pp. 62-63)

Charles Krauthammer says, "I believe that when the point of a terrorist attack is to force the media to function as interpreters, the media have a heavy responsibility not to do the interpreting" (Terrorism and the media, 1984, p. 50). Norman Podhoretz (1980), editor-in-chief of *Commentary*, argues that attempts to explain terrorism are inherent apologia:

> The regnant assumption in the American press concerning the rise of terrorism is that it is rooted in what may be called 'social causes.' . . . It is invariably psychologically the case that explanations of anything in terms of social causes tend to exculpate the thing being explained. (p. 86)

None of the sources is very specific about how a stick-to-facts guideline might take force. It is most often proposed as an individual and voluntary form of self-restraint for news professionals.

Take sides. A second guideline is equally vague and resembles a patriotic call to arms, suggesting that journalists fight terrorism. Charles Fenyvesi, a columnist for the *Washington Post*, calls terrorism a war "in which a reporter must take sides and must determine whether he is interested in preserving life and helping the hostages, or whether he is interested in getting the scoop" (Midgley & Rice, 1984, p. 13). Wilkinson (1978) suggests five ways the press can take part: focusing public concern and support for the authorities, shattering the myth that terrorists champion the oppressed "by showing the savage cruelty of terrorists' violence and the way in which they violate the rights of the innocent"; relaying police warnings and instructions during any emergency; providing a forum to discuss and develop adequate countermeasures, and ensuring that the official response "is consistent with the rule of law, respect for basic rights, and the demands of social justice" (p. 4).

Those who support guidelines suggest that they would alleviate the problem of terrorism: David Hubbard, a psychiatrist who studied and interviewed over 100 hijackers and insurgents, suggests that "if the media cut their coverage down to the importance of other minor news, these men wouldn't act" (Hickey, 1976, p. 6; Hubbard, 1975, pp. 27-32). And Jeremiah A. Denton, chairman of the Senate Judiciary Committee Subcommittee on Security and Terrorism, offers a subtle analysis of the relationship between terrorism and guidelines:

> I am not suggesting that without media reporting, terrorism would cease to exist. Cause and effect are not so vitally linked in this case. . . . Terrorist incidents may not be media-created events but they are undeniably media-promoted events. We can postulate, therefore, that although terrorism is a weapon of the weak, it is self-evident that, deprived of media attention and publicity, terrorism would become a weapon of the impotent. (Midgley & Rice, 1984, p. 10)

The seminar sponsored by the Chicago papers condemned government regulation and called for guidelines (The media and terrorism, 1977, pp. 15-16), and Alexander (1979, p. 169) reported that the *Chicago Sun-Times*, the now-defunct *Chicago Daily News*, the *Courier-Journal*, the *Louisville Times*, United Press International, and CBS News had adopted guidelines. But Salomone (1975) urged the collection of empirical data to indicate "the degree to which any restrictions on the mass media are likely to have a beneficial effect on the control of terrorism" (p. 45). Schmid and de Graaf (1982) again noted the lack of evidence seven years later and said: "Guidelines are introduced on the mere basis of unchecked assumptions. The least the media could do before they accept guidelines is to make sure that the guidelines serve the purpose for which they are meant" (p. 171).

Access

Some observers call on the media to follow a different sort of guidelines. Instead of "just the facts" and "us against them" they would require the exact opposite.

Do more analysis. Some see sticking to facts as part of the problem and suggest a solution: explaining the meanings of terrorist acts. Frank H. Perez, deputy director of the U.S. State Department Office for Combatting Terrorism, argues:

> The U.S. press seems to be mostly event-oriented. Every terrorist event which occurs is reported. You may find it reported in two or three lines on the last page of a newspaper. It is very shallow reporting, lacking any real analysis. Thus the American public is not gaining an appreciation for terrorist events and what they mean. (Midgley & Rice, 1984, p. 19)

This approach would not be uncritical of terrorism or terrorists themselves but would provide greater detail. It also pushes toward greater investigation of both sides of the conflict. Robert Cox (1981), professor of journalism at Harvard University, says that "the media are failing in their duty by not reporting truthfully and not commenting fairly on the terror used to fight terror" (p. 299).

Provide access. Schmid and de Graaf (1982) propose a sort of equal-time regulation. They argue that terrorism is a ploy for media attention that would vanish if all groups had media access, and they suggest world acceptance of a "right to communicate" (p. 170; also see Chapter 5).

Laissez-faire

The vulnerable-media camp generally sees no reason for singling out the media for control. Syndicated columnist George Will declares, "To think that the press holds the key to the problem of terrorism is not uncustomary narcissism on the part of the journalistic profession" (Terrorism and the media, 1984, p. 53). Some journalists flatly oppose any sort of intervention; A. M. Rosenthal, executive editor of the *New York Times*, says that

> the last thing in the world I want is guidelines. I don't want guidelines from the government and I don't want any from professional organizations or

anyone else. The strength of the press is its diversity. As soon as you start imposing guidelines, they become peer-group pressures and then quasi-legal restrictions. (1976, p. 14)

And Kupperman (1979) of the U.S. Arms Control and Disarmament Agency insists that press controls shift but do not reduce terrorism:

As their theatrical presence diminishes, there is little point in their increasing the level of violence. Economic and other institutional forms of disruption are more likely. Targets such as electrical power grids, water systems, commercial aircraft, pipelines, and communications systems are obvious. (p. 60)

A related theory is that coverage of terrorism is naturally self-limiting in the press. Podhoretz suggests that boredom puts a limit on the amount of terrorism coverage audiences will tolerate. In the same seminar, Krauthammer agrees: "Airplane hijackings, for example, are now covered on the inside pages of most newspapers" (Terrorism and the media, 1984, pp. 47-50). After a period of increasing coverage, media attention dies down, regardless of the number of incidents. According to this theory, the more common terrorism is, the less it will be covered.

Summary

There is no consensus among authorities in the field about the relationship between the media and terrorism. Those who posit that media are culpable see a causal link with terrorism that calls for regulation. Their opposites see the media as vulnerable and consider intervention inadvisable. Scholars and journalists themselves seem fairly partisan, although some present arguments from both sides.

The culpable-media model uncovers two dilemmas. The first involves a cycle of coverage: As media cover terrorism, they incite more terrorism, which produces more media coverage. The result is more terrorism. The second dilemma involves a cycle of control: If government or the media censor coverage, the controls tend to harm the credibility of the government and/or the media. The terrorists may stop their acts, but they may be just as likely to resort to even greater violence. Either consequence encourages more control, which results in more terror by the state, the insurgents, or both—and the cycle continues.

The vulnerable-media model presents its own dilemma: Media do not cause but are the victims of terrorism. Controls are counterproductive, and free and competitive media may be naturally self-limiting in their coverage of terrorism. Any control on coverage, even a natural one, will be ineffective because terrorists can shift to other forms of communication by striking vulnerable points in the infrastructure of liberal societies, such as electrical and water systems. In other words, although the mass media are involved, they present no escape from terrorism.

The dispute over whether the media are to blame and should be controlled might be settled by an appeal to hard data. To discover the state of evidence in the field, terrorism research pertaining to a single medium, newspapers, was reviewed. The following summary of the principal quantitative studies in the subfield shows how the disagreement plays itself out in the literature. It also describes the antecedents that might guide research in visual communications.

Part 2: Research on the Press

Violence in the media has been generally examined without singling out terrorist violence (Gerbner, 1988; Jackson, Kelly, & Mitchell, 1977, pp. 227-314). Besides the work by Weimann mentioned previously, other studies focus on the content or terminology of newspapers to examine their coverage of terrorism. Thomas W. Cooper (1988) reported that "the use of the word *terrorism* in journalism usually appears in commentary about *foreign* events or domestic events with *foreign sponsors*" (p. 2). These studies are not essentially visual in their approach to the topic, but they do provide some guidance to visual researchers.

Content Studies

Some research has examined the use of the word *terrorism* and its variants (*terror*, *terrorist*, etc.), along with its absence or the use of other terms in similar contexts, to explore how newspapers cover terrorism.

Epstein

In this category, Edward C. Epstein's (1977, pp. 67-78) research is exemplary. He analyzed the use of the term *terrorism* in the *New York Times*, *Salt Lake Tribune*, and *Los Angeles Times*. He then compared the actual mention of terrorism to all cases where the term could have been used because the newspaper itself had previously applied the label to similar events. The *New York Times* used the term less frequently and was the only newspaper to apply the term to state terrorism (terroristic acts by a government). Epstein considered the use of the term to be

> symbolic of an overall type of press bias found in varying degrees in all of the newspapers studied. The press in the United States may be a free press with respect to absence of external censorship, but is clearly not free from internally-generated bias. This bias, ranging from the "establishment liberal" point of view reflected in the *New York Times* to the "establishment conservative" point of view found in the *Los Angeles Times* and the *Salt Lake Tribune*, demonstrates that the press in the United States normally is a vehicle for orthodox opinion of one kind or another. (p. 76)

The Epstein study skirts the causal relationship between the media and terrorism and deals with the control dilemma only obliquely. His work suggests that an important point in the analysis of control, at least in the U.S. press, is the political position of the individual newspaper, which tends to follow tacit internal guidelines in its treatment of terrorism. His positioning of the three newspapers is based on common knowledge of their politics. The political positions of newspapers might also have explanatory force in studies of the form of their coverage.

Picard and Adams

In Chapter 2, the authors examined the words used to report political violence in the *Los Angeles Times*, the *New York Times*, and the *Washington Post* for a wide range of terms, dividing them into nominal and descriptive characterizations of political violence. Picard and Adams further analyze the use of these terms by media and government sources and by witnesses. Media sources preferred the term *hijacking* (16.6% of 858); government sources favored criminal act

(14.6% of 41). The preponderance of terms used by the media (83% of 1121) and all terms used by witnesses (29) were nominal in character. Government sources used more descriptive terms (56% of 39). The media also used more nominal characterizations of acts (95% of 702) than of perpetrators (61% of 419). Picard and Adams do not speculate on the explanations for these differences, but they did discover that most of the terms were selected by journalists (94.3% of 1189): "This finding means that media quoted primary sources less than 6% of the time. That number is far below what would normally be considered good practice."

Their work appears to show that the media rely only slightly on direct quotation of the individuals involved in terrorism and that their characterization of terrorism is more neutral than that of their government sources. Although these results are related to the issue of news play, Picard and Adams do not explicitly raise that question.

These studies of content present a model that could be explored in parallel by visual research. The form of these stories might be correlated with their content, and the conclusions about the politics and restraint of the press can guide visual researchers. Other studies of terrorism have already ventured in that direction. Besides the analysis of words, some researchers have explored certain aspects of form. Although not thorough examinations of the full range of formal characteristics of news coverage, these studies lay a groundwork and provide preliminary guidance for future work in visual studies.

News Form Analyses

Most of the research on terrorism coverage treats visual and formal aspects only tangentially and not in much detail.

Kelly and Mitchell

Michael J. Kelly and Thomas H. Mitchell (1981, pp. 269-296) compared the coverage of transnational terrorism in the *New York Times* and the London *Times* with an authoritative list of terrorist events from 1968 to 1974 (Jenkins, n.d.). The study examined the space allocated to terrorism coverage in the two newspapers, finding that the New York paper ran more stories and pictures (348 and 182) than its London counterpart (281 and 95), but the London *Times* dedicated slightly more space (13,846 square inches, or roughly 30 pages) than the *New York Times* (13,741 square inches).

The authors also considered the prominence of coverage by its position on the front page or in the upper half of the page (with a headline above the fold), concluding that the London paper played the stories more prominently (31% of the 134 articles on terrorism appeared on page one, and 35 articles with headlines above the fold) compared to the New York paper (20% of 120 articles on page 1, 25 above the fold). (Kelly and Mitchell also rated the picture by whether it illustrated the events themselves or served only as background, but reported no findings.)

The two papers ignored about 44% of the terrorist events selected randomly from the list. Sometimes the omissions reflected a regional preference. For example, many of the terrorist incidents in South America were ignored by both newspapers. And both papers were more likely to report on hijackings, kidnapping, and murder (118, 63, and 66 articles respectively in New York; 85, 52, and 47 in London) than on crimes not involving a threat to persons. Murder and armed attack received the largest average volume of coverage (543 and 242 square inches for New York, 418 and 228 for London). As for the prominence given to stories, armed attack had the greatest share of headlines above the fold (43% in New York, 71% in London).

Kelly and Mitchell also examined the terrorist groups being covered, finding that Palestinians, who committed twice the number of terrorist acts, received 9 times as many articles as South American terrorists in the *New York Times* and 11 times as many in the London *Times*. The articles on Palestinian terrorists in both papers were three times as large as similar articles on South American terrorists. The study went on to explore a specific case in Brazil, following the pattern of the overview just described. Kelly and Mitchell (1981) work squarely within the academic camp that argues that the media are culpable.

> The continuing existence of the terrorist, as well as his credibility, is based on his ability to attract and hold the attention of the news media. The fortunes of the terrorist, like those of the politician, can rise and fall at the whim of the press. (p. 274)

They conclude that "the news media are one of the most important weapons in the terrorist's arsenal." Their study confirms the correlation between extreme events and news play. They found "a notable tendency for the more sensational terrorist tactics to receive rather massive coverage in the Western press" (pp. 288-290).

They consider terrorist acts to be rooted in social injustices that need to be communicated. Their study indicated that "a sizable minority of terrorist incidents go completely unnoticed by the Western media" and that "less than 10% of the coverage in either newspaper dealt in even the most superficial way with the grievances of the terrorists."

Although they are critical of the breadth and depth of coverage, they conclude that the stick-to-facts approach flouts the aims of terrorists.

> Our findings indicate that while transnational terrorism does generate a considerable amount of press attention, the particular type of coverage it receives would appear to undermine the effectiveness of terrorism as a communications strategy. (p. 269)

Paletz, Fozzard, and Ayanian

A 1982 study by Paletz, Fozzard, and Ayanian (1982, pp. 162-171) of coverage in the *New York Times* of three terrorist groups focused mainly on the mention of the names of the groups by specific reporters, but visual measures of space and emphasis were also included. The authors coded the length of the articles in number of lines, and they noted whether the article appeared in a prominent location, which they defined as the first five pages of the first section, the front of the second section, and the first three pages of the "Sunday Week in Review" section. They also indicated whether the articles appeared in news briefs located "near the front" of the newspaper. The terrorist groups were mentioned in a significant share of the articles emanating from their homelands, and two thirds of their acts were prominently placed, according to the authors' definition. The headlines treated violence as the primary theme more often than did their accompanying stories (p. 166).

Paletz, Fozzard, and Ayanian's finding that the media rely on authority sources, confirmed by Adams and Picard (see Chapter 2), casts "further suspicion on the common contention that the media help legitimize violent groups and their activities" (p. 168). The study also found that the more violent acts were more prominently played and that "routine" acts received less space.

> The *differences* in coverage of the three groups, however, appear to be less a result of a group's history or ideology than of the spectacular nature of the acts it committed during the period studied. Violence is news; spectacular violence is big news. (p. 169)

Paletz, Fozzard, and Ayanian (1982) proposed to put "the conventional wisdom and its suppositions to empirical test," and their conclusions support the vulnerable-media model of terrorism (pp. 162, 170). Their study of broadcast media reached a similar conclusion (Paletz, Ayanian, & Fozzard, 1982).

Antecedents

These two studies go beyond the simple content analysis of terms used by Epstein (1977) to explore visual aspects of the presentation of terrorism news. Their work follows in the footsteps of Richard Budd (1964), whose study compared coverage of the United States in four New Zealand and four Australian dailies during three months.

Budd found that an item count and a space measurement were inadequate to describe how the news was presented. He added other measurements: The headline could be coded for the size of its typography and the number of columns it spanned. The story could be considered long not only because of the total space it occupied but also because of its length in a single column. Its position in the newspaper was also a factor. Stories that appeared on the front page of the newspaper or a section, or on the top half of the page, were considered more prominent. Finally, the use of a picture sometimes served as a form of emphasis (also reflected in the total space of the article).

Budd polled newspaper editors on these factors and found a consensus on all but the use of pictures. Editors did not agree on whether using a picture was a factor in their judgment of prominent news play (pp. 259-262). His study points to a visual method of measuring whether stories of terrorism are played more prominently in a newspaper. Prominent play would, under this definition, be significantly different from the norm of all news in the newspaper.

Summary

These studies have explored, whether explicitly or not, the issue of media responsibility for terrorism. They address the charge that newspapers encourage political violence by the way they play the news. Their method has generally been to analyze verbal content, specifically the use of the charged term *terrorism*. Although exaggerated coverage may be contained in the words chosen to describe events, in the angle or slant of the writing, and in the organizational scheme of the account, these prose expressions are not usually the focus of indictments against the press. The literature of terrorism follows a long tradition of accusing the press of bias or sensationalism by implicating the visual form of the report (Juergens, 1966, p. 45). The visual substance of these charges has only recently received attention (LaVoie & Johnston, 1989, p. 10).

So far the content studies have analyzed visual presentation using a variety of measurements, none of them comparable or thorough. Space has been measured in square inches (including pictures) and number of lines (excluding pictures), prominent position has been defined as above the fold (even though inside newspapers, most stories appear high on the page), and prominent location has been assigned to front pages, the first three pages, and the first five pages. The size of the headline has been measured by its typography and column width. But most of the measurements of visual form, including direction, color, and value, have been ignored.

These studies have been inadequate from the perspective of visual studies, but they are pioneers. They point to an important candidate for research in the field of visual communications. Prominent news play is at the crux of the debate over whether the media contribute to terrorism. It suggests a separation of print from broadcast media for investigation as well as the examination of the politics of the media themselves, and it goes to the heart of the debate over control of the media.

Implications for Visual Research

The visual form of news is a measurable phenomenon that includes not only the extent of coverage but also the emphasis each story receives by its position relative to other news. Media directors also have at their disposal a full vocabulary of form to provide emphasis: the abstract qualities of shape, direction, scale, color, and so forth. Together, these formal qualities can be used to compare the coverage of one type of news with another or of the same news in different media outlets. To the degree that such comparisons provide useful data, they may contribute to the debate over terrorism and the media.

Causation

A central issue in the literature is whether the media have some responsibility for terrorism, by encouraging and exacerbating terrorist acts or by spreading terror. One reason for the lack of data to support the causal hypotheses is that research can usually show the presence or absence of factors but cannot firmly establish cause and effect without falling into the *post hoc ergo propter hoc* fallacy. Visual phenomena have the same limitation, and visual research probably cannot supply direct evidence for a causal link to terrorism.

A universal answer to the question of responsibility, for the media and for most or all terrorism, may be elusive. One strategy is to narrow the coverage of each study to specific media and individual cases of terrorism. The reduced scope might then permit a broader analysis from several perspectives. As part of the historical, cultural, and empirical description of an individual case, research on the visual presentation of terrorism news might cast indirect light on the larger issue of cause and effect. As specific studies accumulate, a composite answer to the responsibility question should emerge.

Crossing Media

The research so far has been divided between broadcast and print media, and that distinction also applies to the form of the news. Visual researchers can examine the two spatial dimensions of newspapers and the added dimensions of time and motion in television. It would seem wise at least initially to retain the separation of newspaper from television journalism for visual study, so that their specific relationships with terrorism can be clarified.

But authorities tend to speak of the media in the aggregate, and their generalizations need to be tested. Verbal content is the primary means of comparison, but newspapers and television share many pictorial and formal visual elements as well. The visual aspects common to print and broadcast news could build a second bridge between the media, which might be used in later studies to explore the overall involvement of the media in terrorism.

Prescriptions

Research can use visual qualities to explore the pattern of limits on press or television coverage and to illuminate the question of control. Censorship reduces coverage and has a measurable effect on the form of news. Guidelines may also affect visual form. Sticking to the facts takes arguably less space than expanding coverage with explanation. Once adequately identified and defined, these guidelines would be amenable to visual research, involving as they do a change in the allocation of space, scale, or time in the media.

But some aspects of media control would escape purely visual methods. Guidelines and self-censorship are embedded in the content of news, and the partisan attitudes of reporters require political and ideological examination. The contribution of visual research in cases of censorship or voluntary guidelines would be to establish the form and extent of control. Combined with other methods, visual research might help to show whether censorship succeeds in limiting coverage and whether guidelines for either sticking to or explaining the facts are in fact followed by the media.

News Play

Visual research is a powerful tool to assess the emphasis given to individual news stories. A visual analysis of a single news outlet will indicate whether a specific topic such as terrorism has received significantly greater emphasis than other topics. A pattern of exaggeration can be demonstrated by comparing the visual forms of competing media.

Content—the choice of terrorism terminology used in the media— will continue to be an important aspect of research on news play. But future studies can better address the specific aspects of form, compare the form to the verbal content, and distinguish between routine and exaggerated coverage. No program of study of the media and terrorism would be complete without some analysis of news play.

Research on news play is the greatest potential contribution for visual communications to the field of terrorism. James W. Hoge (1982) has raised "the question of how much air time or how many column inches actually are devoted to terrorism" and found that "there are no empirical data available" (p. 92). Some research outside visual communications has led the way, but thorough and comparable studies not only of the volume but of the other aspects of the form and presentation of news are needed. Visual researchers can advance the study of terrorism by applying their detailed knowledge of form to analyze news play, an important dimension of the complex and baffling phenomenon.

References

Alexander, Y. (1979). Terrorism and the media: Some considerations. In Y. Alexander, D. Carlton, & P. Wilkinson, (Eds.), *Terrorism: Theory and practice* (pp. 159-174). Boulder, CO: Westview.

Bassiouni, M. C. (1981, Spring). Terrorism, law enforcement, and the mass media: Perspectives, problems, proposals. *The Journal of Criminal Law and Criminology, 72,* 1-51.

Bassiouni, M. C. (1982, Spring). Media coverage of terrorism: The law, the public. *Journal of Communication, 32,* 128-143.

Bell, J. B. (1978). *A time of terror.* New York: Basic Books.

Budd, R. W. (1964, Spring). Attention score: A device for measuring "news play." *Journalism Quarterly, 41,* 259-262.

Cooper, H. H. A. (1977). Terrorism and the media. In Y. Alexander & S. M. Finger (Eds.), *Terrorism: Interdisciplinary perspectives,* (pp. 141-156). New York: John Jay.

Cooper, T. W. (1988, July). Terrorism and perspectivist philosophy: Understanding adversarial news coverage. *Terrorism and the news media research project monograph series.*

Cox, R. (1981). The media as a weapon. *Political Communication and Persuasion, 1,* 297-300.

Epstein, E. C. (1977, Spring). The uses of "terrorism": A study in media bias. *Stanford Journal of International Studies, 12,* 67-78.

Galtung, J., & Ruge, M. H. (1970). The structure of foreign news. In J. Turnstall (Ed.), *Media sociology* (pp. 259-298). Urbana: University of Illinois Press.

Gerbner, G. (1988). Violence and terror in the mass media. *Reports and Papers on Mass Communication,* No. 102. Paris: UNESCO.

Gerbner, G., Gross, L., Jackson-Beeck, M., Jeffries-Fox, S., & Signorielli, N. (1978, Summer). Violence on the screen. *Journal of Communication, 28,* 176-207.

Gurr, T. (1970). *Why men rebel.* Princeton, NJ: Princeton University Press.

Hickey, N. (1976). Terrorism and television: The medium in the middle. *TV Guide,* August 7.

Hoge, J. W. (1982). The media and terrorism. In A. H. Miller (Ed.), *Terrorism: The media and the law* (pp. 89-105). Dobbs Ferry, NY: Transnational.

Hubbard, D. G. (1975). A glimmer of hope: A psychiatric perspective. In M. C. Bassiouni (Ed.), *International terrorism and political crimes* (pp. 27-42). Springfield, IL: Charles C Thomas.

Jackson, R. J., Kelly, M., & Mitchell, T. H. (1977). Collective conflict, violence and the media in Canada. *Ontario Royal Commission on Violence in the Communications Industry Report, vol. 5: Learning from the media.* Toronto: Queen's Printer for Ontario.

Jenkins, B. (n.d.) *International terrorism.* Los Angeles: Crescent.

Jenkins, B. (1983). Research in terrorism: Areas of consensus, areas of ignorance. In B. Eichelman, D. Soskis, & W. Reid (Eds.), *Terrorism: Interdisciplinary perspectives* (pp. 153-177). Washington, DC: American Psychiatric Association.

Johnpoll, B. (1977). Terrorism and the mass media in the United States. In Y. Alexander & S. M. Finger (Eds.). *Terrorism: Interdisciplinary perspectives* (pp. 157-165). New York: John Jay Press.

Juergens, G. (1966). *Joseph Pulitzer and the New York World.* Princeton, NJ: Princeton University Press.

Kelly, M. J., & Mitchell, T. H. (1981). Transnational terrorism and the Western elite press. *Political Communication and Persuasion, 1,* 269-296.

Knauss, P. R., & Strickland, D. A. (1988). Political disintegration and latent terror. In M. Stohl (Ed.), *The politics of terrorism* (pp. 85-125). New York: Marcel Decker.

Kupperman, R. H. (1979). Meeting the terrorist threat: Challenges to a free society. *Terrorism: An International Journal, 2,* 58-63.

Laqueur, W. (1977). *Terrorism.* Boston: Little, Brown.

LaVoie, S., & Johnston, A. (1989). Examining the examiner. *AIGA Journal of Graphic Design, 7,* 10-11.

Lazarsfeld, P., & Merton, R. K. (1948). Mass communication, popular taste and organized social action. In L. Bryson (Ed.), *The communication of ideas* (pp. 95-118). New York: Institute for Religious and Social Studies.

Midgley, S., & Rice, V. (Eds.). (1984). *Terrorism and the media in the 1980s.* Washington, DC: The Media Institute.

The media and terrorism [a seminar sponsored by the *Chicago Sun-Times* and *Chicago Daily News*]. (1977). Chicago: Field Enterprises.

Ontario Royal Commission on Violence in the Communications Industry. (1977). *Report, Vol. 3.* Toronto: Queen's Printer for Ontario.

Paletz, D. L., Fozzard, P. A., & Ayanian, J. Z. (1982, Spring). The IRA, the Red Brigades, and the FALN in the *New York Times. Journal of Communication, 32,* 162-171.

Paletz, D. L., Ayanian, J. Z., & Fozzard, P. A. (1982). Terrorism on television news: The IRA, the FALN, and the Red Brigades. In W. C. Adams (Ed.), *Television coverage of international affairs* (pp. 143-165). Norwood, NJ: Ablex.

Picard, R. (1986, Fall) The conundrum of news coverage of terrorism. *University of Toledo Law Review, 18,* 141-150.

Picard, R. G., & Sheets, R. S. (1986). *Terrorism and the news media research bibliography.* Columbia, SC: Association for Education in Journalism and Mass Communications.

Podhoretz, N. (1980). The subtle collusion. *Political Communication and Persuasion, 1,* 84-89.

Rabe, R. L. (1979). Terrorism and the media: An issue of responsible journalism. *Terrorism: An International Journal, 2,* 67-74.

Rosenfeld, S. S. (1975). How should the media handle deeds of terrorism? *Washington Post,* November 21, p. A19.

Salomone, F. (1975). Terrorism and the mass media. In M. C. Bassiouni (Ed.), *International terrorism and political crimes* (pp. 43-46). Springfield, IL.: Charles C Thomas.

Schmid, A. P., & de Graaf, J. (1982). *Violence as communication.* London: Sage.

Schmid, A. P., & Jongman, A. J. (1988). *Political terrorism* (rev. ed.). New York: North-Holland.

Shaw, D. (1976). Editors face terrorist demand dilemma. *Los Angeles Times,* September 15, Part 1, p. 14.

Terrorism and fit news. (1977). *New York Times,* March 15, p. 36.

Terrorism and the media: A discussion. (1984, October). *Harper's Magazine,* pp. 47-55.

United Nations Secretariat. (1975). Sixth committee report, Sept. 27, 1972. In M. C. Bassiouni (Ed.), *International terrorism and political crimes.* Springfield, IL: Charles C Thomas.

Weimann, G. (1983, Winter). The theater of terror: Effects of press coverage. *Journal of Communication, 33,* 38-45.

Wilkinson, P. (1978, Summer). Terrorism and the media. *Journalism Studies Review, 3,* 2-6.

Wilkinson, P. (1986). *Terrorism and the liberal state* (2nd ed). Houndmill's, UK: Macmillan Education.

Index

About the Authors

Paul D. Adams (Ph.D., University of Texas at Austin) is Chairman of the Journalism Department at California State University, Fresno. He has worked as a professional journalist at *The Oregonian* in Portland, Oregon, and at other newspapers and wire services across the country. He previously taught at the University of Texas, Baylor University, and the University of Portland. He is widely published.

A. Odasuo Alali (Ph.D., Howard University) is Assistant Professor of Communications at California State University, Bakersfield. He served on the Non-Daily Newspaper Committee of College Media Advisers and the Journalism Advisory Board at Los Angeles Trade and Technical College. In the summer of 1985, he worked for the *St. Petersburg Evening Independent* as a faculty fellow of the American Society of Newspaper Editors. He is the author of several journal and newspaper articles. He is also author and editor of two books: *Media and Development in Nigeria: A Primer for Policy Makers,* and *Mass Media Sex and Adolescent Values: An Annotated Bibliography and Directory of Organizations.*

Tony Atwater (Ph.D., Michigan State University) is currently an Associate Professor of Broadcast Journalism and Assistant Director of the Michigan State University Honors College. His awards and honors include being named a 1990 Poynter Institute Teaching Fellow and a 1988 Ford Foundation Postdoctoral Fellow. His research has been widely published in referred journals and presented at numerous conferences. He is currently writing *The Living Room Crisis: Social Reality and the Evening News*. He serves on the editorial boards of *Journalism Review* and the *Journal of Mass Media Ethics*.

Kevin G. Barnhurst is Assistant Professor of Journalism at the University of Illinois at Urbana-Champaign. He has been a visiting faculty member for seminars at the Poynter Institute for Media Studies, St. Petersburg, Florida. As a Fulbright scholar in Peru, he lectured at the Universities of Cusco, Piura, and Lima, and has published Spanish language articles on visual communications, graphics, and visual literature in international journals. An active graphic designer, he is the founder of the graphic design program at Keene State College, University System of New Hampshire, where he won a National Teaching Award in graphics/design. He has been a layout and design coach for the *Minnesota Daily* and other newspapers.

Kenoye Kelvin Eke (Ph.D., Atlanta University) is Associate Professor and Coordinator of Political Science at Savannah State College, Savannah, Georgia. His postdoctoral education includes participation in the Summer Institute on Regional Conflict and Global Security at the University of Wisconsin-Madison; and the MIT-Harvard University Summer Institute on Nuclear Weapons and Arms Control. His recent publications include an article in *The Griot*, and a book, *Nigerian Foreign Policy Under the Military Regimes, 1966-1979*. He is currently coediting *Conflict and Cooperation in Intra-African Relations* with Hashim Gibrill. He has served as a consultant for the Florida Endowment for the Humanities (Governor's Conference 1986).

Jack Lule is an Assistant Professor of Journalism at Lehigh University with a specialization in international media studies and criticism. A former contributing writer for the *Philadelphia Inquirer*, he received a Ph.D. in mass communication and the Certificate in Global Policy Studies from the University of Georgia. He has been recognized with several research awards and grants for his work in media criticism. His research has appeared in *Journalism Quarterly*, *Political Communication and Persuasion*, and other journals.

Robert G. Picard (Ph.D., University of Missouri) is a Professor of Communications at California State University, Fullerton. He is project director of the Terrorism and the News Media Research Project of the Association for Education in Journalism and Mass Communication. A specialist in the political communication and controls of information, he has written widely in those fields. He is the author of numerous scholarly articles and author and editor of numerous books including *In The Camera's eye: News Coverage of Terrorist Events* and *Media Portrayals of Terrorism: Functions and Meaning of News Coverage*. He is associate editor of *Political Communication and Persuasion* and a member of the editorial boards of the *International Encyclopedia of Terrorism*, *Terrorism Annual*, and *Journal of Mass Media Ethics*. He has received numerous awards and honors, including the Clinton F. Denman Freedom of Information Award.

Brian K. Simmons (M.A., Pepperdine University) is currently an Assistant Professor of Communication at Saint Joseph's College, Rensselaer, Indiana. His research interests include terrorism and the media, radio subcultures, and media law. He has authored or coauthored several journal articles and book chapters.

John David Viera (Ph.D., J. D., University of Southern California) is Professor of Film at California State University, Long Beach. He is a Visiting Professor at Pennsylvania State University, 1990-1991. A graduate of the London International Film School, he has produced and directed 10 award-winning films and television shorts as well as more than 80 commercials and CLIO-winning PSAs for a variety of clients. His articles have appeared in various journals. His book *Lighting for Film and Electronic Cinematography* is scheduled for publication in 1991. He was cofounder of *The Entertainment Law Journal* and currently is editor of *Entertainment, Publishing and the Arts Handbook*, an annual survey of entertainment and intellectual property law.

NOTES

NOTES

NOTES

NOTES

NOTES

NOTES